MY LIFE ON A PLATE

RECIPES FROM AROUND THE WORLD

Born and raised in Harlem, New York, Kelis Rogers, better known by just her first name, first came to prominence singing the hook of Ol' Dirty Bastard's hit Got Your Money. Years of chart dominating songs and thrilling, boundary-pushing music followed, resulting in millions of albums sold and numerous top 10 hits. She has released six albums, won Brit, Q and NME Awards and has been nominated for two Grammy Awards. Her latest album, *Food*, made with a live band and horn section, mints a sound that is rootsy, raw and soulful without ever being retro. Upon release, the album was praised as one of her most adventurous works yet. Kelis has toured every corner of the world, performed at every major festival and shared the stage with the world's top artists. A fashion icon and designer muse since the early days of her career, she is celebrated for a personal style that is often as creative and forward-thinking as the music she makes. Aside from her career in music, Kelis is a Le Cordon Bleu-trained chef with multiple television cooking specials and a burgeoning entrepreneurial streak with her Bounty & Full organic sauce line. www.bountyandfull.com

This book is for you, Mum.
Thank you for endlessly pouring into
me. I'm proud to be your daughter.

To Knight, I want to leave with you
an abundance of wonderful things,
so this too is for you. I love you.

MY LIFE ON A PLATE

RECIPES FROM AROUND THE WORLD

Kelis

with Carolynn Carreño

Photography **David Loftus**
Illustrations **Hannah Morrison**

KYLE BOOKS

First published in Great Britain in 2015 by
Kyle Books, an imprint of Kyle Cathie Ltd
192-198 Vauxhall Bridge Road
London SW1V 1DX
general.enquiries@kylebooks.com
www.kylebooks.com

10 9 8 7 6 5 4 3 2 1

ISBN 978 0 85783 301 3

Editor: Kyle Cathie
Editorial Assistant: Claire Rogers
Copy Editor: Sarah Scheffel
Angliciser: Jo Richardson
Designer: Anita Mangan
Photographer: David Loftus
Illustrator: Hannah Morrison
Food Stylists: Sophia Green,
  assisted by Sarah Asch & Jessica Vliet
Prop Stylist: Robin Turk
Hair: Maisha Oliver
Make-up: Gaby Torell
Production: Nic Jones, Gemma John
  and Lisa Pinnell
Management for Kelis: Steve Satterthwaite, Geoff Barnett and
Alexis Peluso for Red Light Management

A Cataloguing in Publication record for this title is available from
the British Library.

Colour reproduction by ALTA London
Printed and bound in Slovenia by DZS

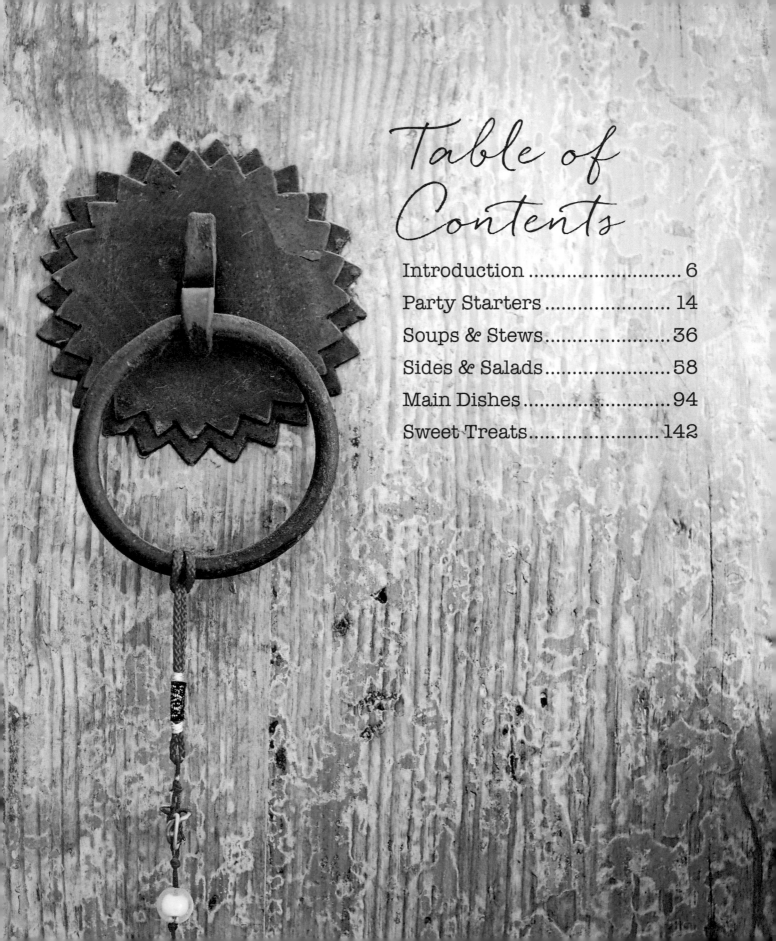

Table of Contents

'Take it all in & kiss it up to the sky'
Bounty & Full

I am my mother's daughter. I can't really say when my love affair with food actually started. I don't even really remember learning to cook. I don't remember learning to sing either, for that matter. But I do remember watching her cook. Every detail was clear and defined. Red lips, red nails, perfume, earrings and a military demeanour that she wore like a royal garment. She was the first chef I'd ever met. When I was growing up she had her own catering and event planning business. There was nothing she couldn't do. I was in the presence of a master. She had a hard working staff but I was always there. I would do anything she asked or she'd let me. I loved the speed, the intensity in the kitchen, the burn and all the hustle and bustle of flowers and platters buzzing by. Not one detail was ever left out. Nothing was ever served at the wrong temperature and it was all always beautiful.

I was born in NY: a native New Yorker and the daughter of a musician and a chef. Get it now? We are what we breathe and eat. At least I am. If you've ever been to my city you'll know that there's barely room enough for everything. But that's why we're so loud. And the food says it all. Little Italy has been reduced to about 2 city blocks of late, but it sits nestled right next to Chinatown. On Sundays after church, sometimes my family would go downtown to Theresa's on Eleventh and First for perogies and kielbasa. I didn't care much then, but I'd eaten my way around the world by the age of eleven on the tiny island of Manhattan. And what a small world it is after all.

I attended LaGuardia High School, better-known back then as the *Fame* school, in the 90s when people were cool and parties were fun. After the club I'd sneak into, we'd go to Third and McDougal for shawarma and falafels at Mamouns, a perfect 3 am snack. I graduated and, before I could even think about my next step, I was signed to Virgin Records for my first album. I went everywhere. I was performing in places I had never even heard of. I was shopping in markets that really were hidden treasures and the food, my friend, the food! It was right before the gentrification of the world, so I've watched it change. Let me explain, though. There was no McDonald's on the Champs Elysées in Paris, and street food in Bangkok was not considered trendy or cool but dangerous and a death wish. Those were the good old days. Travelling still held a sense of prestige and awe. Crossing paths with so many artists and bands along the way, the no-name club in any particular city in any particular country became our Vegas. What happens in (insert anywhere) stays... there. Too young to notice, too stupid to care.

I woke up one morning and ten years had just happened. Just like that. I wasn't strung out or wallowing in self-pity, but it suddenly occurred to me that this was all I had done, and that, even though I recognised it as a blessing, I thought it wise to get off the train for a moment and gain some perspective. It also just so happened that I was, for the first time since I was seventeen, truly a free agent. I wasn't signed and I had no obligations to anyone. Plus, by that point I was habitually irritated and bored with the industry that had raised me.

This story is coming to its point, right now. So here it is: I was sitting in my house in Silver Lake, California at the kitchen counter on Friday afternoon, and I heard a commercial on TV for a culinary school. And, like a cartoon anvil had just been released from the sky, I was hit. Yes, my most brilliant idea yet! That's what I'm going to do next. I'll never forget, I looked up the number for Le Cordon Bleu and within a few minutes it was

decided that I would start the semester full-time bright and early Monday morning.

It is rare that I say this about anything, but as soon as I hung up the phone I was terrified and so nervous: first day of school jitters but on steroids. I was too old for this, and I hadn't had a boss in more than 10 years. Hell, I had just declared how bossy I was to the world with ring tones ricocheting in assorted pre-teen gatherings across this great nation. I certainly had not been in a class setting in even longer than that. So, yes, I was in awe of what I'd done. I wasn't even sure if my brain was still equipped to learn any real valuable information. I thought for sure I had left those brain cells in an ashtray in Istanbul or anywhere many moons ago.

I won't ramble on with any more details about that, but I gotta tell you that something, no, everything changed. I was enthralled. I soon realised that, fear aside, this was one of the best things I would ever do. I wasn't a mother yet so this held steady in its position for a while.

I have always loved talking to the elderly, the ones who are lucid and can keep their story straight, but, more seriously, because it reminds me that it's not over till it's over. And that whether I went on to write my greatest album yet, or never stood

behind a Neumann U87 again, this was just another chapter, and I didn't owe anyone any explanations for running away into the arms of a big, fat kitchen. I was good here. I loved that.

So, blah, blah, blah, and on and on. I did release another album and I went on tour. I started talking pictures of the markets, and slipped away to food adventures when there was no gig, literally eating my way from sea to sea. I've always had a bit of an issue with punctuality, but that was those days and for different reasons we won't speak of here. Then, I was showing up at shows just in the nick of time, and I was so full. The last thing I wanted was to squeeze into that sequinned catsuit. You can't even imagine—there were so many days like that. I was more in the mood for a nap. But that's beside the point. The point is that I love finding the tiniest hole in the wall with the best roti tisu on the southern coast of Penang.

I started taking gigs in cities that made no sense career-wise for my music, but because it was my little secret: I was basically going for a food tour from country to country, often day to day. I had to learn how to detect quickly what was important and what was valuable in each place I visited, so that time was not wasted. It was like developing my own Cliff's Notes or synopsis. Ironically, music and food are the quickest and most sure-fire ways to do that. Tell me what you eat and what you listen to, and I'll tell you who you are. What began happening was that I was taking so many crash courses on each city's food that, naturally, I started to make comparisons and see similarities. What I realised is that, while I may not have been fully focused in Dr. Schneider's history class fifth period, he might have been on to something. You can trace our history through food and cooking techniques if you look closely. We can see where

something originated and how it got here and, for all of our differences, wars and religions, we all started off with the same ideas. There is no real departure between gyoza and empanadas, perogies and samosas. Who doesn't love a whole roasted pig? That crispy skin that you hear crunch and crackle... there's no vegan substitute. And rice stained with the vibrant colour of saffron in Spain (where I had the pleasure to live for the better part of a year) is so similar to the achiote in Puerto Rico where I spent every summer with my family as a child. The food I'm drawn to is the food that tells us who we are and what we are. It can have personality, heartache, and rebirth all on one plate. What better way to tell our story? This is who I am. This is who we are.

I remember, during my first trip to Beirut, being at the house of a friend's friend who had a friend and how I was welcomed into his home and the spread of food completely covered the table. We were planning our day's drive to see the cedars and suddenly I lost what I was planning to say, because, though the words were right there at the tip of my tongue about to trickle out with ease, on its way into my mouth was my first encounter with biryani Saudi-style. Between the heat, the precision of the rice, and the temperature on the patio that night, it was clear I had just met the star of the show. Pleasure to meet you. And, although out of respect it was not appropriate to enjoy a glass of wine at this particular dinner, it didn't stop me from salivating at the memory of my Australian summer and my first introduction into big reds and how perfect, under different circumstances, a full-bodied Shiraz would be with flavours like this.

I can go on and on, and I will as we progress. I want this book to represent life lived casually and abundantly. I have no delusions, there's no reason to recreate the wheel, and I wouldn't dare suggest that I could. However, over the past 15 years, I've been swindled and enchanted by some of what I think are the most tantalizing and yet obvious flavours in the world, and, if I've learned anything from the experiences, it's that the very nature of who we are probably started somewhere, some time, long ago at the bottom of an ancient cast iron skillet much like mine.

Living well. Eating well. Being well is a lifestyle. I believe if we treat our everyday with the same consistency of thought our quality of life is elevated. It doesn't have to be a task; it shouldn't be. I made a list that's ongoing, of things I keep in my home and pantry. So cooking is fun and can be spontaneous.

Here's a list for your start up kitchen. You may already have a lot of these things. It's easy to interchange and play around with recipes once your foundation is laid. You should replenish as you go along but your pantry and kitchen should never be empty. These are just some basics but think about your eating habits and what flavours feel like home to you and add to the list to make it your own. Have fun and buen provecho!

Equipment

Food processor (it can be small but a chef's must-have)

Chef's knife

Cast iron frying pan

A few wooden spoons

Chopping board

Blender

Scales

Potato peeler

Cheese grater

Dairy

Butter

Soured cream

Milk

Whipping cream

Yogurt

In the cupboard

Canned coconut milk

Condensed milk

Evaporated milk

Sugar

Self-raising flour

Baking powder

Baking soda

Vanilla extract

Sea salt

Granulated garlic

Paprika

Cinnamon

Nutmeg

Cayenne pepper

Dried herbs (oregano, thyme, rosemary, basil)

Curry powder

Black pepper (I like to grind my own. I use a coffee grinder)

Bag of brown rice (what I like, but it can be any white rice if you prefer. I also always keep some barley and quinoa in my pantry)

Coarse cornmeal

Rolled dried oats

Wholegrain flour

Fruit & Vegetables

Onions

Garlic

Peppers, red and green

Frozen corn

Frozen fruit (whatever you like)

Stock (vegetable and chicken, you can make your own and store it or buy it. If you buy it make sure it's low sodium)

Beans (dried or canned)

Chickpeas

Crushed tomatoes

Passata (these two ingredients are just good for back up)

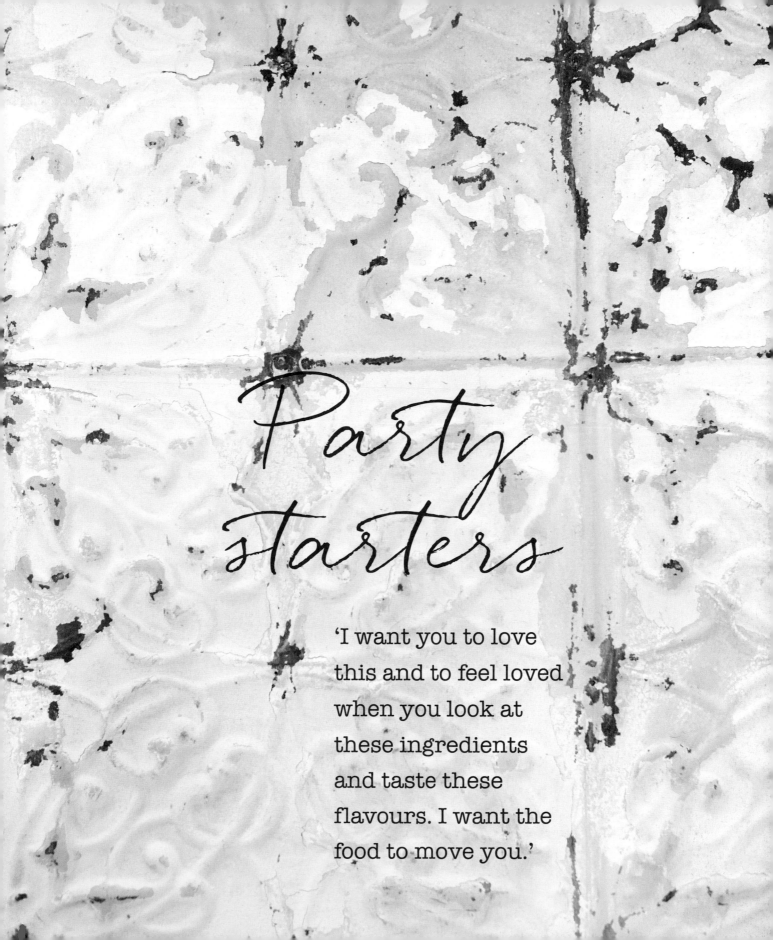

Party starters

'I want you to love this and to feel loved when you look at these ingredients and taste these flavours. I want the food to move you.'

Spinach & Feta Pinwheels

These are spinach pies. They are great for dinner parties. I like to serve them with some wine while I make the finishing touches to the rest of the meal.

MAKES 16 PINWHEELS

2½ tablespoons olive oil

½ yellow onion, finely chopped

¾ teaspoons sea salt

5 garlic cloves, very finely chopped

180g loosely packed fresh spinach leaves

1 tablespoon balsamic vinegar

1 medium egg

1 teaspoon black pepper

75g feta cheese, crumbled

Plain flour for dusting

450g (about 20 sheets) filo pastry, defrosted according to the packet instructions if frozen

115g unsalted butter, melted

1 medium egg beaten with 1 tablespoon water for the egg wash

1. Heat the oil in a medium saucepan on a medium-low heat. Add the chopped onion, sprinkle with ¾ teaspoon of the salt and cook gently, stirring often, for about 10 minutes until the onions are tender and translucent. Toss in the garlic and cook for 1 minute, stirring constantly so that it doesn't burn. Add the spinach and vinegar, season with ½ teaspoon of the remaining salt and cook for about 2 minutes until the spinach is wilted, folding it as it wilts. Drain the spinach mixture through a colander and push on it gently with the back of a spoon to strain out the excess water. Set aside to cool to room temperature.

2. Whisk the egg, pepper and the remaining ½ teaspoon salt in a large bowl. Add the spinach mixture and stir to combine. Gently fold in the feta.

3. Position an oven shelf in the centre and preheat the oven to 180°C/gas mark 4.

4. Dust a flat work surface lightly with flour and lay down one sheet of filo. Brush the filo with some of the melted butter and lay another sheet on top of it. Brush with more butter and continue until you have stacked half of the sheets (about 10) of pastry; do not brush the top sheet with butter. Using a bench scraper and pastry wheel cutter or knife, cut the stacked filo into 5cm squares. Working with one square of filo at a time, make a 2cm cut at a 45-degree angle to each of the four corners. Spoon a heaped tablespoon of the spinach filling in the centre of each square of filo. Fold every other corner inwards, creating a pinwheel shape. Brush the exposed dough with the egg wash and place the pinwheel on an ungreased baking tray. Repeat with the remaining squares of filo, then repeat again with the remaining sheets of filo pastry.

5. Bake the pinwheels on the centre shelf for 5–7 minutes until they are golden brown.

Chickpea Hummus

I live in an area of Los Angeles that has a large population of people from the Middle East and Israel, and hummus is sold in stores and restaurants all over the neighbourhood. Living there, I fell in love with it and now hummus feels like my native cuisine. I make hummus regularly, because it's easy to throw together and it feels like a healthy snack for me and my family. I like to serve it with a really beautiful plate of vegetables, including sliced tomatoes, celery, carrots, cucumbers, and any other delicious vegetables I might have around.

MAKES ABOUT 700G

2 × 400g cans chickpeas, drained

¼ yellow onion, roughly chopped

4 garlic cloves, peeled

180ml olive oil

3 tablespoons fresh lemon juice

1½ tablespoons Dijon mustard

½ teaspoon black pepper

½ teaspoon ground cumin

3 teaspoons sea salt, plus more to taste

1. Put all of the ingredients in the bowl of a food processor fitted with a metal blade and... viola! A delicious and healthy snack! Add more salt to taste.

Black Bean Hummus

I make a bunch of different flavours of hummus, but besides the classic, black bean is my favourite. It's well worth the small amount of time it takes to make your own hummus. Whenever I buy it ready-made instead, I get home and taste it and it's never as tasty as one I whip together myself.

MAKES ABOUT 900G

2 × 400g cans chickpeas, drained

400g can black beans, drained

120ml olive oil

4 garlic cloves, peeled

1 jalapeño pepper, deseeded and roughly chopped

2 tablespoons fresh lime juice

2½ teaspoons sea salt, plus more to taste

½ teaspoon black pepper

1. Put all of the ingredients in the bowl of a food processor fitted with a metal blade and purée. Add more salt to taste.

Prawn Alcapurrias

When I was growing up, we spent every summer with family in Puerto Rico. There's an area there by the sea called Piñones where they sell little snacks, all made with seafood, including prawn alcapurrias. These deep-fried, stuffed grated cassava (some people use green plantains) are amazing and remind me of who I am. They can be filled with meat or seafood.

When graduating from culinary school, for the last project of our chef dissertation they gave us an ingredient, and with that ingredient we had to make something in the French style we'd learned in school… My ingredient was cassava, so I called my mum to ask her how to make alcapurrias. She called my grandmother, who said I wouldn't be able to do them because I didn't have the traditional banana leaves to roll them in. She said how tedious it was, too – I think she didn't want me to make them, or to fail making them. It makes me laugh now. I'm like, 'Geez, thanks for the vote of confidence, Mum'. I think my grandmother made them so well that my mum figured there was just no use in trying. I decided to do it anyway. All the women in my family were holding their breath, thinking I was going to fail, but the alcapurrias were easy enough to roll in my hands. And they turned out amazing! The chewy crunchiness of the cassava is unusual and the spicy flavourful prawn filling is so good. I got an A-plus.

You will have more filling than you need for these; you can use it on top of Smoked Bacon Arepas (page 22), scramble it in eggs, or serve it over brown rice.

MAKES 16–20 PIECES

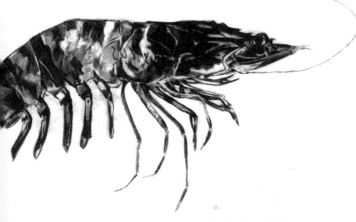

For the cassava coating

2 cassava roots, peeled and grated on a box grater using the microplane side

2 tablespoons Sofrito (page 75)

1 tablespoon Sazón (page 21) or
 1 teaspoon achiote paste plus 1 tablespoon sea salt, crumbled with your fingers

½ teaspoon black pepper

For the prawn filling

2 tablespoons olive oil

½ large yellow onion, very finely chopped

1 teaspoon sea salt

6 garlic cloves, very finely chopped minced

½ green and ½ red pepper, cored, deseeded and very finely chopped

60g Sofrito

1 teaspoon dried oregano

½ teaspoon ground cumin

½ teaspoon black pepper

½ teaspoon cayenne pepper

½ teaspoon achiote paste, crumbled with your fingers

600g raw prawns, peeled, deveined and finely chopped

Rapeseed or vegetable oil for deep-frying

125g plain flour

1. To prepare the cassava coating, put the grated cassava in a piece of doubled-up muslin and squeeze to strain out the excess liquid. Transfer to a large bowl, cover and refrigerate overnight or for several hours. Strain the cassava again through a muslin and squeeze it in your fists to extract as much liquid as possible. Season with the sofrito, achiote paste, salt and pepper and mix to blend the flavours.

2. While the cassava mixture is chilling, make the prawn filling. Heat the oil in a large sauté pan over a medium-high heat. Add the onion, season with ½ teaspoon of the salt and sauté for about 5 minutes until the onion

begins to soften. Toss in the garlic and green and red pepper and sauté for about 5 minutes to soften. Add the sofrito, oregano, cumin, black pepper, cayenne, achiote paste and the remaining ½ teaspoon salt and stir to combine. Add the prawns and cook for about 4–5 minutes until translucent. Remove the pan from the heat and set aside to cool.

3. When you're ready to fry the alcapurrias, heat 7.5–10cm of oil in a large saucepan over a medium heat until the oil reaches 180°C. Meanwhile, strain the cassava mixture through a double layer of muslin again, squeezing it in your fists to extract as much liquid as possible. Prepare a bed of kitchen paper for draining.

4. Put the flour into a shallow bowl. Divide the cassava mixture into 16–20 portions and form each into a patty. Put about 2 teaspoons of the prawn filling in the centre of a patty and close to make a tiny football shape. Coat the ball in the flour. Repeat with the remaining cassava patties. Slide the alcapurrias into the hot oil and deep-fry for 6–8 minutes until they are golden brown and cooked through. Remove from the oil and drain on the kitchen paper. Serve immediately.

Sazón

Sazón, which means seasoning in Spanish, is one of a range of seasoning mixes made by Goya, a brand of Latino foods, which is a key ingredient in our cooking. It's what gives our rice its pretty yellow colour. It's hard to make Puerto Rican food without Sazón. The Goya version is readily available in New York and Los Angeles and anywhere else that there are large populations of Latin people, but if you can't get it, you can make your own using this recipe. You can use achiote (a paste made from annatto seeds) or turmeric.

MAKES ABOUT 250G

75g onion granules

55g garlic granules

12g dried oregano

25g smoked paprika

3 tablespoons plus 1 teaspoon ground coriander

3 tablespoons ground cumin

2 tablespoons plus 1 teaspoon sea salt

1 tablespoon plus 1 teaspoon black pepper

2 teaspoons ground turmeric

1. Pulse all of the ingredients together in a food processor fitted with a metal blade. Store at room temperature in a jar with a tight-fitting lid for up to 3 months.

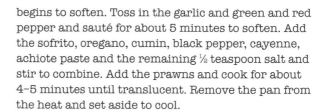

Smoked Bacon Arepas

Many Central and South American cultures make arepas, but these are Colombian. My husband is Colombian, and when we first started dating, he was like, 'I'm going to come over and make you something.' He made it seem like it was this really spectacular culinary extravaganza, which is very cute, because actually this recipe is the easiest thing in the world! And really delicious. As a consequence, I fell in love with arepas, and I fell in love with him. Colombian arepas are really thin, so they aren't cut in half like a lot of arepas are. I like bacon in my dough, but you can also use spring onions or sweetcorn. Arepas have been completely integrated into our family cuisine, which is nice. I make a bunch of them and then throw one in the toaster for a snack for my son. You can top them with all kinds of stuff: white cheese, Ají (page 45), avocado, soft chorizo, a fried or scrambled egg. Asking me what you can put on an arepa is like asking someone what you can put on bread…

Traditionally, Colombian arepas are cooked on a grill but I also give you directions for cooking them in a frying pan, which is more convenient.

INGREDIENT NOTE: Harina Venezolana is a speciality Colombian product which you can get from a speciality market or the internet.

MAKES 12 AREPAS

510g masa harina Venezolana (pre-cooked white cornmeal), such as Harina P.A.N Blanco

½ teaspoon truffle salt

1.6 litres boiling water

200g smoked bacon rashers, fried and chopped

2 tablespoons rapeseed oil, or more as needed (if you're cooking the arepas in a frying pan)

350g queso cotija, crumbled (you can substitute feta or Spanish white cheese)

1. Put the masa and the salt in a large bowl. Slowly pour in the boiling water, mixing with wooden spoon to form a dough. Knead the dough a few times while it's still in the bowl to form a ball.

2. Scoop up about 70g of the dough, press in some of the bacon and shape the dough into a disc that's about 1cm thick and 7.5cm across.

3. Preheat a grill to a medium-low heat, or heat the oil in a frying pan over a medium-low heat. Cook the arepas on the barbecue or in the frying pan for 6–8 minutes per side until golden brown, turning them only once.

4. Crumble the cheese and whatever topping you are putting on the arepas. Sprinkle with a little salt depending on choice of topping and serve.

Spinach & Chickpea Fritters with Yogurt Cucumber Sauce

When I was in high school, my friends and I used to go to a little hole in the wall called Mamoun's Falafel in the Village at three in the morning for falafel pittas. I've been hooked on falafel ever since. These fritters are inspired by falafels but they're lighter and fluffier. They're smaller than traditional falafel, about the size of ping pong balls.

MAKES ABOUT 46 FRITTERS

2 × 400g cans chickpeas, drained

30g fresh spinach leaves

¼ large yellow onion, roughly chopped

3 tablespoons plain flour

3 garlic cloves, smashed and roughly chopped

1 fresh dill sprig, roughly chopped

1½ teaspoons sea salt

½ teaspoon black pepper

¼ teaspoon ground sage

¼ teaspoon ground coriander

Rapeseed or vegetable oil for deep-frying

1 recipe Yogurt Cucumber Sauce (see below)

1. Place all the ingredients in the bowl of a food processor fitted with a metal blade and purée to create a smooth batter, then transfer to a mixing bowl.

2. Heat 7.5–10cm of oil in a medium saucepan over a medium heat until the oil reaches 180°C. Prepare a bed of kitchen paper for draining the fritters.

3. Spoon out 1 tablespoon of batter, shape it into a ball with your hands and then flatten it to make a little disc. Drop the disc into the oil and continue to shape and add more little discs of batter to the pan, frying each fritter for about 5 minutes until golden brown. Remove each fritter from the oil when it is done, transferring it to the kitchen paper to drain, and continue to shape and add more discs to the pan. When all of the fritters are fried, sprinkle them with salt. Serve warm, with the yogurt sauce on the side.

Yogurt Cucumber Sauce

I served this as part of a lunch feast at home in LA. It was actually a business meeting, but I figured since we were all together, we should make a day of it. I was thinking summer in the Mediterranean, so I made Spinach and Chickpea Fritters (see above), whole baked sea bass, tomatoes, and this yogurt sauce. The sauce was meant specifically for dipping the fritters, but it went with everything on the table. You can also serve this sauce with grilled lamb, and I use it to make sandwiches on fresh-from-the-oven pitta bread that I buy in my neighbourhood.

MAKES ABOUT 475G

360g natural Greek yogurt

35g finely chopped cucumber

2 tablespoons very finely chopped yellow onion

2 garlic cloves, very finely chopped

1 tablespoon fresh lemon juice

1 teaspoon sea salt

1. Stir all of the ingredients together in a medium bowl until thoroughly combined. Cover and refrigerate until ready to serve.

Japanese Sweet Potato Samosas

One of the things I love about travelling is connecting the dots in terms of how different cultures eat. What I've learned is that people are all the same and, sometimes, we all want to eat the same things. Deep-fried dough is one of those universal things. They can be stuffed with meat or potato or veggies, whether you call them samosas, pirogies, gyoza, ponchiks, empanadas or dumplings, they're delicious.

I was working in Singapore, staying at the Marina Bay Sandy Hotel. Underneath the rest of the building is the mother load of food courts. It's magnificent! There I had this incredible chutney-flavoured doughy textured dumpling. We did not speak the same language, but what joy that dumpling brought me. It was a perfect sweet potato. These samosas remind me of that day.

MAKES 32 SAMOSAS

1 teaspoon sea salt, plus more for boiling and seasoning

900g Japanese (yellow-fleshed) sweet potatoes or satsumaimo, peeled and cut into large chunks

2 carrots, cut into a small dice

2 teaspoons curry powder

½ teaspoon ground cumin

½ teaspoon ground coriander

65g frozen petit pois, defrosted

1 recipe Buttery Flaky Everything Dough (page 157)

Rapeseed or vegetable oil for deep-frying

1. Bring a large pan of water to the boil and salt it to taste like the ocean. Add the sweet potatoes and boil for about 15 minutes until tender. Put the carrots in a sieve and, 1 minute before the potatoes are done, dunk the sieve into the water to blanch the carrots. Remove the sieve and set aside. Drain the sweet potatoes in a colander, transfer them to a large bowl and mash with a potato masher. Add the curry, cumin, coriander and salt and mash to distribute the seasonings. Fold in the carrots and peas. Season with more salt to taste.

2. Divide the dough into 16 equal-sized (about 40g) balls. Roll each ball out to create a round about 10cm across and 3mm thick. Fold one corner over the middle and fold the second corner over so that the edges meet. Pinch to seal the edges, creating a round cone with the top open. Spoon 1 heaped tablespoon of the filling into the cone and pinch to close. Put the samosa on a baking tray and continue shaping and filling the remaining samosas until you have used up all of the dough and filling. Transfer all of the samosas to the baking tray.

3. Heat 7.5cm of oil in a large saucepan over a medium heat until the oil reaches 180°C. Prepare a bed of kitchen paper for draining the samosas.

4. When the oil is hot, put as many samosas in the oil as will fit comfortably and fry for 6–8 minutes, turning to cook evenly, until golden brown and crispy. Remove the samosas from the oil and drain them on the kitchen paper. Let the oil return to 180°C, then fry the remaining samosas in the same way. Serve immediately.

Papas Rellenas

Papas rellenas, which means 'stuffed potatoes', are popular in Peru, Chilli, Cuba, Columbia and, of course, Puerto Rico. They are potato balls filled with picadillo, a seasoned minced meat mixture, and then deep fried. When I see papas rellenas in New York, they're huge, like softballs. In LA, they're tiny, like golf balls. Who knows why there's a difference; I make mine about the size of a tennis ball. You can serve these as an appetiser or a meal; two or three would make a great dinner. You'll have picadillo leftover after making the papas rellenas. Serve it on top of brown rice, bulgur wheat or mashed potatoes.

MAKES 12 PAPAS RELLENAS; ABOUT 1.35KG

For the picadillo

2 tablespoons olive oil

3 tablespoons Sofrito (page 75)

1 large yellow onion, very finely chopped

3 teaspoons sea salt

1 teaspoon ground black pepper

2 garlic cloves, finely chopped

1 large heirloom or vine-ripened tomato, diced

900g beef mince

1½ tablespoons smoked paprika

1½ teaspoons dried oregano

1 teaspoon ground cumin

45g small pimento-stuffed olives, cut in half

For the potatoes

450g Yukon gold or Maris Piper potatoes, peeled and cut into large chunks

Sea salt for the boiling water

360ml soda water

125g plain flour

Rapeseed or vegetable oil for deep-frying

1. To make the meat filling, heat the oil in large frying pan over a medium-high heat. Add the sofrito and cook it for 1 minute. Add the onion and season with 1 teaspoon of the salt and ½ teaspoon of the pepper. Reduce the heat to medium and cook, stirring often, for about 10 minutes until the onion is tender and translucent. Scatter the garlic into the pan and cook for about 1 minute until it's fragrant, stirring so that it doesn't brown. Add the tomato and its juices and cook for 3–4 minutes until it begins to break down. Add the beef mince and break it into small pieces with a spatula or wooden spoon. Sprinkle with the paprika, oregano, cumin, the remaining 2 teaspoons salt and the remaining ½ teaspoon pepper. Cook for about 5 minutes until the meat is no longer pink, stirring often. Stir in the olives and cook for about 2 minutes to meld the flavours. Set aside to cool to room temperature.

2. To prepare the potatoes, bring a large pan of water to the boil and salt it to taste like the ocean. Add the potatoes and cook for about 20 minutes until they are tender and crumbly but not mush. Drain the potatoes in a colander and transfer them to a large bowl. Smash the potatoes with a potato masher to crumble but not completely mash them. Set the potatoes aside or put them in the fridge to cool to room temperature. (Cooling the potatoes helps the papas rellenas stay crispy and whole when fried.)

3. Divide the potato mixture into 12 pieces and shape each into a patty as thin as you can with your hands. Put 1 heaped tablespoon of the picadillo in the centre of a patty and roll the potato around it to form a round ball about the size of a tennis ball. Put the ball on a baking tray. Repeat with the remaining potato patties.

4. Combine the soda water and flour in a medium bowl and whisk to break up any lumps.

5. Heat 7.5–10cm of oil in a large saucepan over a medium heat until the oil reaches 180°C.

6. One at a time, dip half the papas rellenas in the batter and carefully drop them into the oil. Fry for 4–5 minutes until golden brown and crispy. Remove with a slotted spoon and place on kitchen paper to drain. Batter and fry the remaining papas in the same way. Serve warm.

Shredded Beef Sliders with Root Beer Espresso BBQ Sauce

I started making these when I had a food truck at South by Southwest music and film festival in Austin, Texas, to showcase my new line of sauces. The meat is a version of ropa vieja, or 'old clothes', which is braised, shredded flank steak traditional to many cuisines of the Caribbean. My mum makes ropa vieja all the time; she taught me to make it. To utilise my barbecue sauce, I got the idea to toss ropa vieja with the sauce and then use the meat to make sliders. You can also serve the meat (with or without sauce) with rice, which is how Puerto Ricans traditionally eat ropa vieja, or use it to fill pastelitos, which are the Puerto Rican version of empanadas, or meat pies, using Buttery Flaky Everything Dough (page 157) for the pie cases. It's good with rice or leftover mashed potato, too. You can use Bounty & Full Wild Cherry BBQ sauce for this, which is how this dish originated.

MAKES 16 SLIDERS

6 sprigs of fresh thyme

4 sprigs of fresh oregano

2 sprigs of fresh rosemary

900g skirt steak, cut into 2 pieces to fit in your pan

1 tablespoon sea salt, plus more to taste

¾ teaspoon coarsely ground black pepper

2 tablespoons olive oil

2 medium yellow onions, roughly chopped

1 green and 1 red pepper, cored, deseeded and roughly chopped

15 garlic cloves, peeled

1 teaspoon smoked paprika

½ teaspoon ground cumin

120ml Root Beer Espresso BBQ Sauce (page 33, or shop-bought)

16 small brioche buns, cut in half

115g unsalted butter, melted

1. Wrap the thyme, oregano and rosemary in a doubled piece of muslin and tie it closed with kitchen string to make a herb bouquet.

2. Season the meat on both sides with the salt and pepper.

3. Heat the oil in a large saucepan or flameproof casserole dish over a medium high-heat for about 3 minutes until it's searing hot. Add one piece of meat to the pan and sear it for 5–7 minutes per side until it is deep brown on both sides. Remove the meat from the pan and sear the second piece of meat. Leave the second piece of seared meat in the pan and return the first piece to the pot, too. Add the herb bouquet, onions, green and red peppers, garlic, paprika, cumin and enough water to just cover the meat and vegetables. Bring the water to the boil over a high heat, then reduce the heat to low, cover the pan and simmer for about 2 hours until the meat can be gently torn apart with a fork. Turn off the heat and leave the meat to cool to room temperature in the liquid.

4. Lift the meat out of the liquid and shred it back into the pan with the cooking liquid. (I like to go at it with kitchen scissors.) Remove the herb bouquet and stir in the barbecue sauce. Season to taste with salt.

5. Brush the insides of the buns with the melted butter and toast the insides only under the grill. Scoop an equal quantity of the barbecue beef onto each bun and serve.

Root Beer Espresso BBQ Sauce

MAKES ABOUT 710ML

2 tablespoons olive oil

1 yellow onion, roughly chopped

4 teaspoons seat salt, plus a pinch (or more to taste)

8 garlic cloves, roughly chopped

60ml distilled white vinegar

2 vine-ripened tomatoes, chopped

250g ready-made tomato pasta sauce

120ml American-style mustard

220g soft light or dark brown sugar

180ml root beer

2 tablespoons balsamic vinegar

2 tablespoons molasses

2 teaspoons pure vanilla extract

3 tablespoons honey

1 tablespoon finely ground espresso coffee

1 teaspoon black pepper, plus more to taste

1 teaspoon ground paprika

1 teaspoon chilli powder

½ teaspoon cayenne pepper

½ teaspoon ground allspice

¾ teaspoon garlic powder

½ teaspoon ground cumin

1. Combine the oil and onion in a large saucepan over a medium-low heat.

2. Sprinkle with 1 teaspoon of the salt and cook about 10 minutes until the onion is tender and translucent, stirring often so that the onion doesn't brown.

3. Add the garlic and the pinch of salt and sauté for 1-2 minutes until the garlic is fragrant, stirring constantly so that it doesn't brown.

4. Add the white vinegar, increase the heat to medium-high and cook for 1 minute, scraping up the brown bits on the base of the pan.

5. Toss in the tomatoes and cook, stirring occasionally, for about 5 minutes until they break down. Add the tomato sauce and mustard and bring the liquid to a simmer.

6. Stir in the brown sugar and cook for about 3 minutes until it dissolves. Pour in the root beer, balsamic vinegar, molasses and vanilla.

7. Bring the liquid to the boil. Reduce the heat and simmer for 15-20 minutes; you're cooking to bring out the sweetness of the tomatoes.

8. Set aside to cool slightly. Transfer to the jug of a blender and purée for about 5 minutes until smooth. Return the purée to the saucepan.

9. Stir in the honey, along with the espresso, black pepper, paprika, chilli powder, cayenne, allspice, garlic powder, cumin and the remaining 3 teaspoons salt. Simmer on low, covered, for 40 minutes-1 hour until the sauce is a deep reddish brown. Taste and add more salt and pepper as needed. Store this in the fridge and it will last for weeks.

Soups + Stews

'I don't know that there is
anything more honest than food.'

Tomato Basil Bisque

For all of the food I love, for all the places I've been, and, having thought about recipes that stand out for me as both a chef and a human being for this book, it occurs to me I really am an American – and I'm very proud of that. My cooking is American in style and with an American flair. American cooking is very distinctive and, as far as soup goes, I think tomato bisque soup and a grilled cheese sandwich is right up there with apple pie; it is as American as you can get. It's just good food, simple and to the point, and exactly what you want. I do eat a lot of soup, but this in particular speaks so much to who I am.

MAKES ABOUT 1.4 LITRES; SERVES 4

60g unsalted butter

1 medium or large yellow onion, diced

3 teaspoons sea salt, plus more to taste

10–12 garlic cloves, smashed and roughly chopped

900g heirloom or vine-ripened tomatoes, cooked and puréed in a food processor or blender

¼ teaspoon black pepper

5 large fresh basil leaves

4 dried bay leaves

1 sprig of fresh rosemary

1 sprig of fresh thyme

2 sprigs of fresh oregano

1½ tablespoons smoked paprika

710ml low-salt chicken stock or water

240ml whipping cream

1. Melt the butter in a large saucepan over a medium heat.

2. Add the onion, season with 1 teaspoon of the salt and cook for about 10 minutes until tender and translucent, stirring often so that the onion doesn't brown.

3. Add the garlic and cook for about 2 minutes, stirring constantly, until it is fragrant and golden brown.

4. Stir in the puréed tomatoes and season with the remaining 2 teaspoons salt, the pepper, basil, bay leaves, rosemary, thyme, oregano and paprika. Cook for 5–10 minutes to meld the flavours and cook off the raw flavour of the tomatoes.

5. Pour in the chicken stock, increase the heat to high and bring the soup to the boil. Reduce the heat and simmer the soup for 15–20 minutes until the tomatoes are really broken down.

6. Stir in the cream and cook for about 3 minutes, just long enough to warm it. Season with more salt to taste. Remove and discard the herbs. Serve warm.

Plátano Soup

Green (unripe) plantains aren't sweet. They don't taste like bananas, but more like potatoes. This soup is rich and hearty and all you will want after eating it is a good, cosy nap.

MAKES 1.9–2.4 LITRES; SERVES 4–6

2 smoked ham hocks or 1 knuckle end, bone-in, halved (about 900g in total)

1.3kg green plantains (7 or 8 plantains), peeled and cut into large pieces

2 large yellow onions, diced

8 garlic cloves (about half 1 head of garlic), smashed

1 tablespoon sea salt, plus more to taste

3 sprigs of fresh thyme

2 long sprigs of fresh oregano

¾ teaspoon ground cumin

Freshly ground black pepper, to taste

200g Ají (see page 45), to serve

1. Put the ham hocks in a large saucepan and add enough water to cover by 5–7.5cm. Bring the water to the boil over a high heat, reduce the heat and simmer the ham for 1 hour, skimming off the foam that rises to the top.

2. Add the remaining ingredients, except the Ají, and boil for about 1 hour 15 minutes until the plantains are tender.

3. Turn off the heat, remove the ham hocks and set aside to cool to room temperature.

4. Purée the soup with a stick blender and add more salt to taste.

5. Pull the meat off the bones, chop it and stir it into the soup, with a little left over to decorate each serving. Top with a spoonful or two of Ají and serve warm.

Butternut Squash Soup

I love this soup. It's funny – for the Food Network cooking show, we'd bought tons of butternut squash to decorate the set and I thought, 'What feels like winter?'. Winter vegetables and, of course, lots of pumpkins. Between the prop person and my mum being obsessed with white pumpkin – my mum was there too – we went to the store and cleaned them out; we got every pumpkin and squash they had. We put them all over the house and put bows on them. When the show was over, I had all this squash, and of course I had to cook it. After a couple weeks of squash this and squash that, my husband and my son were like, 'Please, no more!'. But there was more. I hate wasting food. We're a member of a vegetable collective that delivers locally grown produce once a week. During the fall and winter months, every single week, there's another butternut squash in our package.

This butternut squash soup was one of the last squash things I made before the season for them was over, and it was such a victory. Even though they were sick of squash, my husband and son both ate it: it was that good. I add cream to the soup but it's also delicious without it.

MAKES ABOUT 3.8 LITRES; SERVES 8

2 butternut squash (about 1.8kg), peeled, seeds removed and cut into 4cm cubes

1 large Spanish onion, sliced

5 sprigs of fresh sage

5 sprigs of fresh thyme

3 sprigs of fresh rosemary

3 dried bay leaves

1 tablespoon ground ginger

2 cinnamon sticks

4 whole cloves

¼ teaspoon freshly grated nutmeg

2 tablespoons sea salt, plus more to taste

75g demerara sugar

2 teaspoons curry powder (preferably hot curry powder)

300ml whipping cream (optional)

Flaked almonds, lightly toasted, for garnish

Currants or black raisins for garnish

1. Combine the squash, onion, sage, thyme, rosemary, bay leaves, ginger, cinnamon sticks, cloves, nutmeg and salt in a large saucepan. Add enough water to cover by 2.5–5cm and bring the water to the boil over a high heat.

2. Reduce the heat and simmer for 10–15 minutes until the squash is mushy.

3. Turn off the heat and use a stick blender to purée the soup.

4. Add the sugar and curry powder and stir until the sugar dissolves.

5. Stir in the cream, if using. Season with more salt to taste. Serve warm, garnished with the almonds and dried fruit.

Three-Bean Soup with Ají

Beans are such a staple in Latino cooking; they're something we're known for eating. This hearty, spicy bean soup is something I make all the time using whatever beans I have to hand. It's something I feel good about making for my son, because it's so healthy and nourishing. I often make it with homemade beef stock that I make from marrow bones, because my son has eczema and marrow is supposed to be good for it. I use a lot of different types of beans. They take a long time to cook, but the good news is that once you get everything in the pot, you can pretty much leave it alone on the hob. It will make the house smell great. The soup is spicy already, but I spoon Ají (page 45) on each serving just to give it that extra kick. In the recipe, I call for you to soak the beans, but I often don't plan ahead enough to do this. If you don't soak them, they will need to be cooked for longer than the time given here.

MAKES ABOUT 2.8 LITRES; SERVES 6–8

700g assorted dried beans (such as cannellini, black, kidney, pinto, moro, scarlet runner beans), soaked overnight and drained

1 tablespoon Sazón (page 21)
or ½ teaspoon achiote paste, crumbled with your fingers

1 tablespoon dried basil

2 tablespoons sea salt, plus more to taste

1 teaspoon black pepper

¼ teaspoon cayenne pepper

4 dried bay leaves

2 red and 1 green pepper cored, deseeded and diced

1 poblano chilli, cored, deseeded and diced

1 Anaheim chilli (aka California green chilli or chile verde), cored, deseeded and diced

3 large tomatoes, diced

2 tablespoons Sofrito (page 75)

3 carrots, thinly sliced

Ají (page 45), to serve

1. Put the beans in a large saucepan with enough water to cover. Bring the water to the boil over a high heat, reduce the heat and simmer the beans for about 30 minutes until they just begin to soften.

2. Stir in the achiote, basil, salt, black pepper, cayenne and bay leaves and cook for about 1 hour until the beans are very tender.

3. Stir in the red and green peppers, poblano and Anaheim chillies, tomatoes and sofrito and cook for about 10 minutes to soften the vegetables.

4. Add the carrots and cook for about 5 minutes until they just begin to soften. Season with more salt to taste and serve this soup on a cold day, with a spoonful of ají topping each bowl.

Ají

Ají is a spicy sauce made of fresh tomatoes and peppers. It's really big in South America. My husband, a Colombian, introduced me to it. It's so easy to make. Just throw everything into a food processor or blender and, in no time, you have an unbelievably fresh, spicy sauce. I make a big batch and keep it in a Mason jar in the fridge. I like to have it on hand to spoon into soups such as Three Bean Soup with Ají (page 42) and Platano Soup (page 38), or with beans, on Smoked Bacon Arepas (page 22), eggs or tacos.

There's almost nothing it's not good on – except dessert. I can't have tacos without it now. When I went to make it for the first time, my husband and I argued about what was the right way. Then I called his mother and she told me how to do it. I use hers as a base for mine, but of course I had to make it my own. I'm grateful to her, because my husband… well, let's say he was confused. Puerto Ricans eat something called mojo de ajo that I grew up eating. My sister was a foreign exchange student in Argentina and she became obsessed with chimichurri. When my husband first told me about ají, I thought it couldn't be that different than mojo de ajo and chimichurri, but it is. And I'm hooked.

MAKES ABOUT 825G

2 habanero chillies, stems removed and roughly chopped (seeds included)

60ml distilled white vinegar

Leaves and tender stems of 1 bunch of fresh coriander, roughly chopped

½ large Spanish onion, roughly chopped

1 bunch of spring onions, trimmed and roughly chopped

4 garlic cloves, smashed and roughly chopped

2 tomatoes, roughly chopped

1 tablespoon sea salt

1 teaspoon black pepper

Juice of 1 lime

1. Put the chillies and vinegar in the bowl of a food processor fitted with a metal blade and pulse to finely chop the chillies. Add the coriander, onion, spring onions, garlic, tomatoes, 2 tablespoons water, the salt, pepper and lime juice. Pulse to a chunky consistency and serve. It will keep in the fridge in an airtight container almost indefinitely.

Coconut Curry Crab Soup

When working on this book, I served this, along with about a dozen other dishes, to a crowd of hungry friends to get their feedback. Everyone loved it! It couldn't be any simpler to make: it's just coconut milk seasoned with lemongrass, curry, and curry leaves, and fresh whole crabs. I don't serve it with rice or anything else; the beauty is in the simplicity. It's so good it's ridiculous.

One of the things about Balinese food is that, if it's crab, there's a whole crab on the plate. Abundance. I love it. It's the entire thing, they might serve it to you with the crab shell being the bowl. It's beautiful. There's something really lush about it that I liked.

INGREDIENT NOTE: Curry leaves, which are integral to Indian cooking, are available at larger supermarkets and Indian and Middle Eastern food stores. You can find lemongrass, one of the most important flavourings in Thai and Vietnamese cooking, in larger supermarkets and Asian groceries.

SERVES 4

5 × 400ml cans coconut milk

2 lemongrass stalks, cut in half lengthways (see Ingredient Note)

1 fresh curry leaf (see Ingredient Note)

2 tablespoons curry powder

1 tablespoon ground ginger

1 tablespoon sea salt, plus more to taste

4 cooked whole small crabs (or use langoustines if small crabs are unavailable)

225g cooked white crabmeat

1. Combine the coconut milk, lemongrass, curry leaf, curry powder, ground ginger and salt in a large saucepan over a medium heat and warm until the coconut milk begins to bubble. Reduce the heat and simmer for about 10 minutes to infuse the coconut milk with the flavourings.

2. Add the whole crabs and heat through for about 5 minutes. Season with more salt to taste.

3. To serve, use tongs to put one crab in each soup bowl. Pour the coconut curry broth over the crabs. Spoon an equal quantity of the crabmeat on top of each serving. Dig in and enjoy!

Corn Chowder with Crabmeat

Chowder is a classic American dish, but rather than using flour, which is the traditional way of thickening chowder, I add puréed corn and reduce the cream with potato, which releases its starches. This makes for an extra rich and delicious soup that also happens to be gluten free. My mum used to make this for me, and now I make it for my son.

Much like rice is in Asia, corn was the backbone of the Americas for a long time. Living in California, we have access to fresh corn most of the year. Using frozen corn is okay too. I love how versatile it is; there are so many things you can use it for. If given the chance I could write a book about corn.

MAKES 2.3 LITRES; SERVES 4–6

Kernels cut from 4 corn cobs or 250g frozen sweetcorn kernels

1.2 litres vegetable stock

60g unsalted butter

1 medium yellow onion, diced

4 teaspoons sea salt, plus more to taste

3 garlic cloves, very finely chopped

1 large Maris Piper potato, scrubbed and diced

1 carrot, diced

6 sprigs of fresh thyme

240ml whipping cream

½ teaspoon black pepper

225g cooked white crabmeat

1. Purée half of the sweetcorn with 240ml of the vegetable stock in a blender or food processor fitted with a metal blade. Set aside.

2. Melt the butter in a large saucepan over a medium heat. Add the onion, season with 1 teaspoon of the salt and cook for about 10 minutes until tender and translucent, stirring often so that the onion doesn't brown. Add the garlic, season with another teaspoon of salt and cook for about 2 minutes, stirring constantly, until it's fragrant and golden brown. Stir in the potato, carrot, thyme and the remaining 2 teaspoons salt. Add the remaining vegetable stock, the puréed corn and the reserved sweetcorn kernels. Bring the soup to the boil, reduce the heat and simmer for about 20 minutes until the soup has thickened slightly and the diced potato is cooked through. Stir in the cream and pepper and cook for about 2 minutes, just to warm the cream. Season with more salt to taste.

3. To serve, spoon some crabmeat into the centre of each bowl, dividing it evenly. Pour the soup into the bowls at the table.

Chinese Short Rib Soup

My mum used to make an Asian roast pork soup that I loved. This soup, which starts with beef short ribs rather than pork, is a cross between hers and the short rib soup I get in Korea Town in Los Angeles whenever I go to the fabulous Korean spa. (The whole time I'm getting scrubbed down, I'm thinking about what I'm going to eat and drink afterwards: short rib soup and boba, or 'bubble tea' – the tea has about 1,800 calories, but I'd say the soup makes up for it!) Cook the soup and noodles separately and serve with the noodles on the side so they don't get soggy and overcooked in the hot broth.

INGREDIENT NOTE: Be sure to buy short ribs on the bone; the bone adds so much flavour to the broth.

SERVES 4–6

900g beef short ribs (see Ingredient Note), cut across (rather than parallel to) the bone and then into 5–6cm pieces containing one bone each

240ml soy sauce

1 large yellow onion, roughly chopped

5 garlic cloves, very finely chopped

1 red jalapeño pepper, stem removed and quartered (with seeds)

1 lemongrass stalk (see Ingredient Note, page 46), cut in half lengthways

2 tablespoons peeled, grated fresh ginger (use a Microplane grater)

60ml honey

Handful of spring onions, trimmed and thinly sliced on the bias (white and green parts)

Sea salt

400g dried vermicelli rice noodles

1. Put the short ribs in a large pan with a lid. Cover the ribs with water and bring to the boil over a high heat.

2. Add the soy sauce, onion, garlic, jalapeño, lemongrass, ginger, honey and spring onions. Return the liquid to the boil, reduce the heat, cover the pan and simmer for about 3 hours until the short ribs are fork tender. Taste for seasoning and adjust if necessary.

3. Turn off the heat and leave the ribs to cool slightly in the liquid. Just before serving, cook the noodles according to the packet instructions.

4. Serve the ribs and broth warm in shallow bowls, with the noodles on the side.

Lentil & Sausage Stew

I serve these lentils really thick, so they're more like a stew than a soup. If you like heat, the lentils are delicious made with spicy Italian sausage. I go to the butcher's and just ask what they've got – maple smoked, Italian smoked, whatever's fresh. Pork is always the most flavourful. I season the sausage meat with cumin, but just a little. Cumin has a really wonderful and distinctive flavour, but it can demolish a dish if you use too much. One tip I have for using spices such as cumin (I'd put nutmeg in the same category) is to smell it first. Smelling it will remind you of how pungent it is, and will help prevent you from over-using it.

I've spent a lot of time in Asia, in places like Kuala Lumpur and Penang, where they cook lentil dishes such as dahl, but I wanted to cook them with flavours that I was familiar with, like the rosemary and the sausage, that remind me of living in Italy and going down to Naples. Lentils are not really pricey, but go a long way, and we ate a lot of them!

MAKES ABOUT 1.6 LITRES; SERVES 4–6

3 tablespoons olive oil

225g pork and herb sausages,
   meat removed from the skins

1 yellow onion, diced

½ fennel bulb, cored and diced

3 teaspoons sea salt, plus more to taste

450g dried green lentils

710ml low-salt chicken stock

2 large carrots, diced

1 red pepper, cored, deseeded and diced

5 garlic cloves, very finely chopped

1 teaspoon black pepper

½ teaspoon ground cumin

4 whole cloves

1 celery stick, diced

1. Heat the oil in a large saucepan over a medium-high heat. Crumble in the sausage meat and cook until it's brown all over, breaking it into small pieces with a wooden spoon.

2. Add the onion and fennel, season with 1 teaspoon of the salt and cook for about 10 minutes until the vegetables begin to soften and the onion is translucent.

3. Add the lentils and chicken stock and bring the stock to the boil over a high heat.

4. Add the carrots, red pepper, garlic, black pepper, cumin, cloves and the remaining 2 teaspoons salt. Cover the pan, reduce the heat to low and for simmer for about 30 minutes until the lentils are soft.

5. Uncover the pan, stir in the celery and serve.

Beef & Bacon Chilli

I make chilli often because I make cornbread often (see Frying Pan Cornbread with Candied Ginger, page 147), and I love a piece of cornbread with chilli poured on top. There's a lot of bacon in this chilli, and there's nothing wrong with that. The fat rendered from the bacon is used to sauté the onions and other veggies. It's ridiculously rich and delicious. I sometimes make chilli with bison instead of beef; trying different meats that I see at the butcher's is fun, just for the sake of trying something new.

MAKES ABOUT 2.8 LITRES; SERVES 8–10

450g streaky bacon, chopped

1 large yellow onion, diced

900g beef mince

2 teaspoons smoked salt (or sea salt
  plus ½ teaspoon liquid smoke),
  plus more to taste

1 teaspoon ground black pepper

½ red and ½ green pepper, cored, deseeded
  and diced

2 large vine-ripened tomatoes, diced

1 bunch of spring onions, trimmed and
  finely chopped (white and green parts)

3 garlic cloves, very finely

2–3 tablespoons chilli powder,
  plus more to taste

2 tablespoons smoked paprika

½ teaspoon cayenne pepper

2 dried bay leaves, crumbled

120ml bourbon

2 × 400g cans red kidney beans, drained

800g passata

1 litre low-salt chicken stock or water,
  or as needed

Graded Cheddar or
  Gouda cheese for serving

1. Cook the bacon in a large saucepan or flameproof casserole dish over a medium heat until the fat is rendered and the bacon is cooked through.

2. Drain the bacon on kitchen paper.

3. Add the onion and mince to the pan. Season with 1 teaspoon of the smoked salt and the pepper and cook, breaking up the meat with a spatula, for about 10 minutes until the meat is cooked through.

4. Add the red and green peppers, season with the remaining 1 teaspoon smoked salt and sauté for about 10 minutes until the vegetables are tender, stirring often so that they don't brown.

5. Add the tomatoes and spring onions and cook for about 5 minutes until the tomatoes break down.

6. Toss in the garlic and sauté for about 2 minutes until it is fragrant. Sprinkle the chilli powder, smoked paprika, cayenne and bay leaves into the pan.

7. Stir in the bourbon, beans and half of the passata and simmer for about 10 minutes.

8. Pour half of the chicken stock into the pan and bring it to the boil over a high heat. Reduce the heat and simmer the chilli for about 1 hour 30 minutes, adding the remaining passata and stock when more liquid is needed and stirring often.

9. Season with more smoked salt to taste. Chop the bacon and stir it into the chilli to rewarm it. Serve in bowls with the grated cheese sprinkled on top.

Oxtail Stew

This stew is so easy to make: you just throw all the ingredients in a pot and cook it for eternity until the meat is falling off the bone. Oxtail stew is easy to turn into oxtail ragù, which can be served over pasta.

I love it and it's funny to me that things that used to be considered peasant food, like oxtail, have recently received a new appreciation from restaurants and chefs around the world. I grew up eating oxtail and nothing compares.

SERVES 4

1.8kg oxtail

2 tablespoons sea salt

1 red and 1 green pepper, cored, deseeded and diced

2 yellow onions, diced

6 garlic cloves, smashed

1 tablespoon smoked paprika

120ml balsamic vinegar

1 tablespoon each of fresh rosemary, thyme and oregano

1 tablespoon black pepper

1. Put the ingredients in a large saucepan or flameproof casserole and add water to just cover the oxtail.

2. Bring the water to the boil over a high heat. Reduce the heat, cover the pan and simmer the oxtail, for about 3 hours until the meat is falling off the bones.

3. Turn off the heat and leave to cool to room temperature in the gravy. Pick the meat off the bones and return it to the gravy; discard the bones. Serve warm.

Oxtail Poutine

A twist on my French-Canadian comfort food favourite, my version replaces French fries with cassava fries and smothers them in meat and gravy from the Oxtail Stew recipe below.

SERVES 6

1 large cassava root (about 270g), peeled and chopped into 2.5cm-long strips

Rapeseed or vegetable oil for deep-frying

¼ teaspoon salt for sprinkling, or to taste

1 litre Oxtail Stew (see above)

60g Manchego cheese, grated

60g Gruyère cheese, grated

60g mature aged Cheddar cheese, grated

1. Bring a medium saucepan of lightly salted water to the boil over a medium-high heat, add the cassava and cook for about 5 minutes until soft. Drain and set aside.

2. In another medium pan, heat 5cm of oil over a medium-high heat until the oil reaches 180°C. Prepare a bed of kitchen paper for draining the fries.

3. Add the cassava strips to the hot oil and flash-fry them until gold and crispy on all sides. Immediately transfer the cassava to the kitchen paper to drain and salt them liberally. (Cassava is very starchy, so it's important that this is done straight away.)

4. Transfer the hot fries to a platter, spoon the oxtail stew on top (be sure to include both shredded meat and gravy) and sprinkle the grated cheeses all over. Serve immediately.

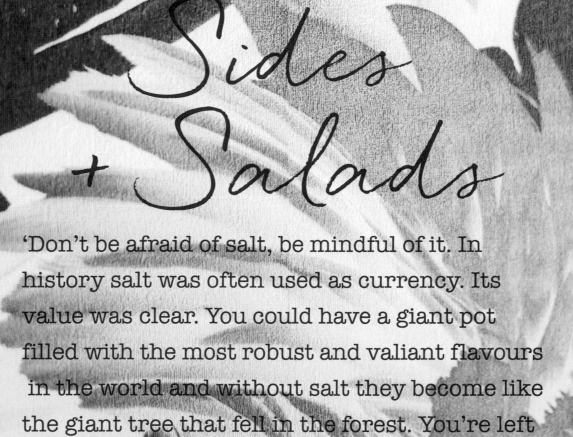

Sides + Salads

'Don't be afraid of salt, be mindful of it. In history salt was often used as currency. Its value was clear. You could have a giant pot filled with the most robust and valiant flavours in the world and without salt they become like the giant tree that fell in the forest. You're left only with the question, "Where is the proof that anything truly happened?"'

Matthew 5:13–16

Fried Red Cabbage

Even though I love them, I didn't grow up eating collard greens, because my mum hates them. Instead, she made variations of cabbage, which is more Caribbean than collard greens are. The purple of the cabbage is a gorgeous colour – it's like art on a plate – and it looks so pretty with the other Thanksgiving side dishes, which tend to be different shades of brown. I often top the cabbage with a big dollop of mascarpone or goat's cheese. The dish looks really pretty that way, and I love the contrasting temperatures of the warm cabbage and the cold, creamy cheese.

SERVES 4–6

115g unsalted butter

1 small yellow onion, diced

1 tablespoon sugar

2 teaspoons sea salt, plus more to taste

½ teaspoon black pepper, plus more to taste

1 red cabbage, about 900g, halved, cored and very thinly sliced

Mascarpone or goat's cheese for garnish (optional)

1. Melt the butter in a large deep frying pan or cast-iron pan over a medium heat.

2. Add the onion and sprinkle with the sugar, along with 1 teaspoon of the salt and ¼ teaspoon of the pepper. Sauté, stirring often, for about 10 minutes until the onion is tender and translucent.

3. Fold in the sliced cabbage and season with the remaining salt and pepper. Increase the heat to high and sauté the cabbage for 10–12 minutes, gently tossing it so that it cooks evenly, until the cabbage is soft and brown around the edges.

4. Season with more salt and pepper to taste. Top with the mascarpone or goat's cheese, if you are using it, and serve.

Chorizo Date Stuffing

Even though my mother is my first and biggest influence when it comes to cooking, she is a die-hard traditionalist to the end, whereas I like to deviate. When I started cooking, my mother let me take over the making of Thanksgiving stuffing. That was a long time ago. Now I like to add chorizo, because chorizo and dates are a great match. I start with rustic, wholegrain bread, which gives great flavour and texture to the stuffing. The bread puffs up in the oven like a soufflé, and the top gets crunchy and golden brown. I'm very particular about texture, and don't want to eat something with the texture of wet bread; this is the opposite. A lot of people cut the crusts off bread when making stuffing, but I leave it on – I like the different texture it adds to the stuffing.

SERVES 8

60g unsalted butter,
    plus more for greasing the dish

450g day-old, rustic, wholegrain bread,
    cut into 2–2.5cm cubes

6 large Medjool dates, chopped

225g hard cured chorizo, finely diced

225g pork and herb sausages,
    meat removed from the skins

1 medium Spanish onion, finely chopped

1 tablespoon plus 1 teaspoon sea salt

1 medium red pepper, cored, deseeded
    and finely chopped

1 medium green pepper, cored, deseeded
    and finely chopped

1 celery stick, finely chopped

1 large carrot, finely chopped

4 garlic cloves, very finely chopped

1 litre low-salt chicken stock

10g fresh flat-leaf parsley or coriander,
    finely chopped

1. Position an oven shelf in the centre and preheat the oven to 180°C/gas mark 4. Grease a 2.8-litre baking dish and set aside.

2. Scatter the bread cubes on two large baking trays and toast them in the oven for about 5 minutes until they're dry and golden. Set the pans aside to cool the bread to room temperature.

3. Transfer the bread cubes to a large bowl. Add the dates and toss to distribute. Set aside.

4. Meanwhile, melt half of the butter in a large sauté pan over a medium heat. Add the chorizo and sausage meat and sauté, breaking up the sausage meat with a wooden spoon or spatula, for about 10 minutes until the sausage meat is crumbled and golden brown. Add the onion, red and green peppers, celery, carrot and garlic. Season with half of the salt and cook, stirring occasionally, for about 10 minutes until the vegetables are soft and the onion is translucent. Add the remaining butter and stir until it melts. Stir in the chicken stock. Add the bread cubes and dates and the remaining salt and gently stir to coat the bread cubes with the vegetable mixture.

5. Transfer the stuffing to the prepared baking dish and spread it out so that the top is even. Sprinkle the parsley or coriander over the stuffing. Cover the baking dish with foil and bake on the centre shelf for 30 minutes. Remove the baking dish from the oven, remove the foil and bake for about a further 30 minutes until the top is golden brown and a skewer inserted into the stuffing comes out clean. Leave the stuffing to cool for 10–15 minutes before serving.

Aubergine & Asparagus with Five-Spice Plum Sauce

My dad was a vegetarian for most of my life. For my father, my mom used to cook a lot of dishes with aubergine, because it has a meaty quality that makes vegetable dishes more hearty. I made this dish inspired by those memories, and by the cute baby aubergine that I saw in the market one day. Whenever I see baby aubergines, I look for a way to cook them. For this dish, the aubergine and asparagus are stir-fried and then tossed in plum sauce. Serve with Duck Fried Quinoa (page 101), plain steamed black rice or Himalayan red rice.

INGREDIENT NOTE: If you can't find baby aubergines, substitute 2 large aubergines, cut in half lengthways and each half cut into 6 or 8 wedges.

SERVES 6

1 tablespoon toasted sesame oil

8 baby aubergine, quartered (see Ingredient Note)

1 bunch of asparagus, stems ends broken off at their natural breaking point, cut into 4cm pieces

2 teaspoons sea salt

3 shallots, thinly sliced

1 tablespoon very finely chopped garlic

70g raw cashews

180–240ml Five-Spice Plum Sauce (see below)

1. Heat the oil in a large sauté pan over a medium heat. Add the aubergine and asparagus, season with 1½ teaspoons of the salt and cook for 4–5 minutes, stirring, until the aubergine begins to brown. Sprinkle the shallots and garlic into the pan, season with the remaining ½ teaspoon salt and cook for about 2 minutes until the shallots are tender and translucent. Add the cashews and enough plum sauce to coat the aubergine, tossing to combine. Serve warm.

Five Spice Plum Sauce

This is my version of hoisin sauce. I toss it into stir-fries and always serve it with Peking Duck (page 103).

MAKES ABOUT 480ML

600ml orange juice (preferably with pulp)

370g stewed prunes, stoned, plus 60ml of their juice

200g granulated sugar

2 tablespoons rice wine vinegar

1 tablespoon Chinese five-spice powder

1 tablespoon very finely chopped garlic

1 teaspoon black pepper

1. Combine all the ingredients in a saucepan and bring to the boil over a high heat. Reduce to medium heat and simmer for about 15–20 minutes until the prunes split and the liquid starts to brown. (Don't cook so long that the sugar burns.) Set aside to cool slightly. Transfer to the jug of a blender or the bowl of a food processor fitted with a metal blade and purée until smooth.

Brussels Sprouts with Currants & Almonds

Even though I'm a total carnivore, my body definitely craves green vegetables, and Brussels sprouts are one of my favourites. I'm sure everybody's mum made their own version of Brussels sprouts, but none of them were very exciting back then. Now Brussels sprouts are really trendy and people are preparing them in all kinds of delicious ways. I cook mine with coconut oil. I also toss in some almonds and dried currants just to keep things interesting, but it's the coconut oil that makes it. The sweet flavour of the coconut oil with the bitter taste of the Brussels sprouts is an unexpected combination, but it's like they were meant to be together. Another thing I like about coconut oil, besides the flavour, is that it's not greasy. I never get tired of them.

SERVES 4

3 tablespoons coconut oil

450g Brussels sprouts, prepared and cut in half lengthways

Sea salt and black pepper

35g shallots, finely chopped

1 tablespoon finely chopped garlic

1 tablespoon currants

1 tablespoon flaked almonds

1. Heat a large sauté pan over a medium heat for about 1 minute. Add the oil and leave to heat up and melt for about 30 seconds until a pinch of salt sizzles when dropped into the pan.

2. Add the Brussels sprouts, cut side down, and season with salt and pepper. Cover the pan and cook the sprouts for about 5 minutes until the faces are dark brown and caramelised.

3. Remove the lid, scatter the shallots and garlic around the sprouts, season them with salt and pepper and give the pan a good shake to distribute the ingredients and turn the sprouts. Cook for a minute or two, uncovered, to soften the shallots and garlic, shaking the pan or stirring the vegetables to make sure they don't burn.

4. Stir in the currants and almonds until well combined. Serve warm.

Butternut Squash & Sweetcorn Casserole

I find that when people are looking for a starchy side dish, they automatically turn to potatoes or rice, but squash has such great flavour and it's also such a beautiful colour – it shouldn't be overlooked. I love butternut squash so much that I could go on and on about all the things you can do with it, but here's a good one. The sweet squash and the savoury onion in this recipe make for a rich and delicious side dish.

SERVES 6-8

1 butternut squash, about 900g, peeled, seeds removed and cut into 2.5cm cubes

½ yellow onion, diced

Kernels cut from 1 corn cob or 65g frozen sweetcorn kernels

1 tablespoon sea salt

½ teaspoon black pepper

½ teaspoon ground cinnamon

1 teaspoon sugar

¼ teaspoon ground cloves

1 teaspoon dried oregano

240ml whipping cream

25g pecans, lightly toasted and chopped

110g Gruyère cheese, grated

1. Position an oven shelf in the centre and preheat the oven to 180°C/gas mark 4.

2. Combine all of the ingredients except the cheese in a large (23 × 33cm) casserole dish. Cover the dish with foil and bake the casserole on the centre shelf for 30 minutes.

3. Remove the dish from the oven, lift off the foil and sprinkle the top of the casserole with the cheese. Bake the casserole, uncovered, for about a further 30 minutes until the squash is fork tender and the cheese is golden brown and melted.

Plantain Mash

Plantains are a fruit in the banana family that are eaten cooked in many different cultures. This plantain side dish makes a really nice, unusual alternative to mashed potatoes; the plantains are boiled until they're soft, drained, and then mashed with butter, cream, garlic and salt. Reserve the cooking liquid from the plantains and keep it in the fridge or freezer to use when making rice, thinning a sauce like that in my Jumbo Shrimp with Salsa Criolla and Strawberries (page 133), or in place of water or chicken stock when making soup. The idea of saving cooking water is also something they emphasised in culinary school: they teach you that everything has value and I try to throw away as little as possible.

INGREDIENT NOTE: When shopping for sweet plantains, look for yellowish-black ones. The blacker they are, the better. Green plantains are not as sweet.

SERVES 4

1 teaspoon sea salt, plus more for the boiling water and to taste

5 sweet yellowish-black plantains, about 1.6kg, peeled and cut in half crossways (see Ingredient Note)

480ml whipping cream

3 garlic cloves

115g unsalted butter, softened at room temperature

½ teaspoon black pepper, plus more to taste

1. Bring a large pan of water to the boil over a high heat and salt it to taste like the ocean.

2. Add the plantains, return the water to the boil and boil for 10–15 minutes, depending on the ripeness of the plantains, until the plantains are very soft when pierced with a fork.

3. Meanwhile, warm the cream over a low heat.

4. Sprinkle the garlic cloves with a big pinch of salt and finely chop and crush them to a paste. (Salt helps to break down the structure of the garlic, making it easier to crush.)

5. When the plantains are done, drain them, reserving the cooking water for another use, and return the plantains to the pan. Reduce the heat to low, add the butter and garlic paste and then mash the plantains with a potato masher to break them up. Add 360ml of the warmed cream and continue mashing until the mixture is creamy, adding more cream if it seems too dry. Season with more salt and the pepper to taste, mashing them in to distribute the seasonings evenly.

Baked Cheese Grits

You may or may not realise that grits and polenta are essentially the same thing. Whether you call them grits or polenta, the issue I have with them is that they spread all over the plate when they're served. Baking grits solves that problem. Also, since I add eggs to the grits before baking them, they puff up in the oven so they're almost like a soufflé, which is nice. I usually make these grits as a side dish to go with Shrimp Etouffée (page 135).

SERVES 6–8

40g unsalted butter, melted and cooled to room temperature, plus cold butter for greasing the baking dish

1½ teaspoons sea salt, plus more to taste

140g grits (coarsely ground cornmeal or polenta)

240ml full-fat milk

2 medium eggs, lightly beaten

240ml whipping cream

180g Cheddar cheese, grated

1. Position an oven shelf in the centre and preheat the oven to 180°C/gas mark 4. Grease a soufflé dish or deep casserole dish and set aside.

2. Bring 710ml water and the salt to the boil in a medium saucepan over a medium-high heat. Gradually add the grits, whisking constantly, until no clumps remain. Reduce the heat to medium and simmer, stirring frequently, for about 5 minutes until the grits are thick and creamy. Whisk in the milk.

3. Whisk 240ml of the grits into the beaten eggs and pour the egg and grits mixture back into the pot, stirring constantly. Stir in the cream, melted butter and cheese until thoroughly incorporated. Season with more salt to taste.

4. Pour the grits into the prepared baking dish and bake on the centre shelf for about 45 minutes until the grits are golden brown and puffed up. Serve warm.

Carrot & Yam Soufflé

You often hear people say that there's no such thing as American food, but that's just not true. Candied yams, for instance, baked with marshmallows on top, is as American as it gets. I made this side dish, which is a cross between candied yams and carrot soufflé, for a 'holiday feast' themed cooking show for television. I ate something similar to this at a little restaurant in Georgia, where I lived for a while, where old grannies go after church. Once I discovered it, it's where I went every Sunday after church, too. The ladies who work there are old and often grumpy. When I would ask them about different things on the menu, they would never give me an answer. They would just say, 'Little girl, do you want it or not?'. I always wanted it, whatever it was. They served a carrot and yam soufflé but they would never tell me how to make it, so I would just order it every week and pick it apart to try to figure out how it was made. This is my version.

Before you do the marshmallows, make a crumble with 115g butter, 2–3 tablespoons (maybe more) of flour, and 100g sugar. Add pecans, if you like them. When the soufflé is almost done, put this on top, then at the very end add the marshmallows. The three different textures together are really spectacular.

SERVES 10

170g unsalted butter, melted, plus cold butter for greasing the baking dish

3 large sweet potatoes, about 900g, peeled and roughly chopped

5 large carrots, about 350g, roughly chopped

240ml whipping cream

200g demerara sugar

4 large eggs, lightly beaten

65g plain flour

1 tablespoon ground cinnamon

2 teaspoons freshly grated nutmeg

1½ teaspoons baking powder

¼ teaspoon sea salt

300g miniature marshmallows

1. Position an oven shelf in the centre and preheat the oven to 180°C/gas mark 4. Grease a 23 × 28cm baking dish and set it aside.

2. In the bowl of a food processor fitted with a metal blade, finely chop the sweet potatoes and carrots on high speed. Add the cream, sugar, eggs, flour, cinnamon, nutmeg, baking powder and salt and pulse to combine.

3. Pour the batter into the greased baking dish and spread it evenly with a rubber spatula. Bake on the centre shelf for 15 minutes.

4. Remove the soufflé from the oven and scatter the marshmallows over the top. (If doing the version to the left. Scatter the prepared crumble, then top with the marshmallows.)

5. Return the soufflé to the oven for a further 15–20 minutes until the soufflé has puffed up and the marshmallows are golden brown. Serve warm.

Arroz con Gandules

When I started travelling as a musician, I realised that, whether it's risotto in Italy, fried rice in China, or paella in Spain, every culture has a seasoned, coloured rice dish with flavourful ingredients. Arroz con gandules, rice with pigeon peas, is 'mine'. A staple of Puerto Rican cuisine, arroz con gandules is something we as a family identified with. But, whereas some families eat arroz con gandules every day, or at least five days a week, for us it was a special treat because my mom, being a chef, was always cooking up new and different things. It's a simple side dish, but it's very flavourful and it looks beautiful. If you make Pernil (page 110), reserve the cooking liquid from the roast and use it in place of water to make this rice.

INGREDIENT NOTE: Gandules, also called pigeon peas, are a legume common in Caribbean cuisine. You can get fresh gandules at Latino grocery stores, particularly where there are large populations of Jamaicans, Puerto Ricans and Dominicans. If you can't find gandules, use frozen green peas or butter beans instead.

SERVES 8

60ml plus 2 tablespoons extra-virgin olive oil

125g Sofrito (page 75)

½ large yellow onion, very finely chopped

2½ teaspoons sea salt, plus more to taste

425g can green pigeon peas, drained and rinsed (you can substitute frozen or canned garden peas; see Ingredient Note)

370g long-grain white rice

3 tablespoons Sazón (page 21) or ¼ teaspoon achiote paste (crumbled with your fingers)

½ teaspoon black pepper, plus more to taste

710ml low-salt chicken stock (or reserved juices)

1. Heat the oil in a large cast-iron pan or 5.7-litre saucepan over a medium-high heat. Add the sofrito and onion, sprinkle with ½ teaspoon of the salt and sauté, stirring often, for about 10 minutes until the onion is tender and translucent.

2. Add the peas and sauté for 2 minutes, stirring often.

3. Add the rice, achiote, pepper and the remaining 2 teaspoons salt and cook, stirring often, for about 3 minutes until the rice is lightly browned.

4. Pour in the chicken stock (or a combination of the stock and the reserved juices from a pork roast). Bring the liquid to the boil over a high heat, reduce the heat to low and simmer, covered, for about 20 minutes until the rice is tender.

5. Uncover the pan, add more salt and pepper to taste and fluff up the rice with a fork.

Sofrito

Sofrito, in Latin cuisine, is different from Italian sofrito. It's a mixture of garlic, coriander, onions, and peppers, all blended up. Sofrito recipes, in my culture, are almost like heirlooms. It's one of the things that every Latin mother has that she wants to pass down to her kids. I have a dear friend who is Dominican, and the conversation that we bonded on was that our mums both used to make sofrito and leave it in our freezers for us. To this day, my mum will come over and make a big batch; it's like she's saying, 'Now you're okay'. Everybody makes sofrito a little differently. This is based on my mother's sofrito, but she doesn't have an actual recipe, and I don't remember ever actually learning to make it.

I freeze sofrito in Tupperware, but some people freeze it in ice cube trays and then pop a sofrito cube out of the tray when they need it.

MAKES ABOUT 720G

2 red peppers, cored, deseeded and roughly chopped

1 large Spanish onion, roughly chopped

80g fresh coriander leaves and stems

80g fresh flat-leaf parsley leaves and stems

20g fresh oregano leaves and stems

15–20 garlic cloves (50g or the cloves from 1 head), peeled

3 tablespoons distilled white vinegar

1 teaspoon sea salt

½ teaspoon ground cumin

1. Purée all of the ingredients in the bowl of a food processor fitted with a metal blade until smooth. (If you use a blender instead, add the herbs halfway into the process of puréeing the ingredients.) Sprinkle over the zest and bake in the preheated oven at 140°C/gas mark 1 for 5 minutes just to dry out a little. Transfer the sofrito into small airtight containers and refrigerate for up to 1 week, or freeze for up to 3 months.

Truffle Wholewheat Mac & Cheese

When I was pregnant, I started trying to be more conscious about what I was putting into my body. I'm not a dieting kind of person, but wanted to eat well. I started baking my own bread (what can I say: I had a lot of time on my hands!). I also started cooking with and eating things like flaxseed (linseed), wholegrains and brown rice. I had also just graduated culinary school. All I wanted to do was stay at home and cook things that were delicious and good for me. This mac and cheese, made with wholewheat penne and four types of flavourful cheese, came out of that period of my life, and now I'm known for my mac and cheese. If I were to ask my husband's friends, my friends, and my family what they want me to make them for dinner or for a birthday, hands down they'd say, 'a pan of your mac and cheese'.

COOK'S TIP: It's important to cook the pasta just until al dente for this recipe. The pasta will continue to cook when it bakes in the oven, and mac and cheese is definitely best when the pasta still has some bite to it.

INGREDIENT NOTE: Truffle salt is a luxurious but handy product consisting of sea salt mixed with black truffle shavings. You can find it at speciality food stores and cheese shops. If you can't locate it, a drizzle of truffle oil is a good substitute.

SERVES 10

½ tablespoon sea salt, plus more for the pasta water

450g wholewheat penne

480ml full-fat milk

240ml whipping cream

225g soured cream

85g unsalted butter, plus more for greasing the pan

65g plain flour

350g extra-mature Cheddar cheese, grated

115g smoked mozzarella cheese, grated

225g Gouda cheese and 115g Havarti cheese, grated

½ tablespoon truffle salt (see Ingredient Note) or a drizzle of truffle oil

1 jalapeño pepper, stem removed, deseeded and very finely chopped

1 sleeve of Ritz crackers (about 100g)

25g unsalted butter, melted

1. Preheat the oven to 190°C/gas mark 5. Grease a 23 × 33cm baking dish and set it aside.

2. Bring a pan of water to the boil and salt it well. Cook the pasta until al dente. Drain and set aside.

3. Infuse the milk, cream and soured cream in a medium saucepan over a medium-low heat until it begins to steam, but don't allow it to boil. Set aside.

4. Melt the butter in a large saucepan over a low heat. Stir in the flour and cook, stirring constantly, for 2–3 minutes. Gradually pour in the milk mixture, whisking constantly until no lumps remain. Reserve 30g each of the Cheddar and mozzarella. Add all the remaining cheeses to the milk mixture, along with the truffle salt and jalapeño, and stir until the cheeses have melted completely. Add the cooked pasta and toss to combine. Transfer to the prepared baking dish and smooth the top to make it as level as possible.

5. Put the Ritz crackers in a bowl and crush them with your hands. Add the melted butter and stir to combine. Sprinkle the cracker mixture over the casserole, followed by the reserved cheeses. Bake for 35–40 minutes until the top is golden brown.

Vegetable Buckle

I was performing and doing the New Year's Eve countdown in Kraków, Poland – it was hilarious and nerve-wracking. An hour before the performance, the producers told me that I had to say 'Happy New Year' and do the countdown in Polish. I had no time to practise, and there I was in front of 140,000 people, standing next to the president of Poland. I managed to get the words out. The next day, with my nerves intact, I had my first savoury pancake, which inspired this buckle.

SERVES 8-10

For the vegetables

3 tablespoons olive oil

175g baby potatoes, cut into 5mm-thick slices

2½ teaspoons sea salt

⅛ teaspoon cayenne pepper

1 teaspoon dried thyme

1 carrot, cut into 5mm-thick slices

1 large yellow onion and 35g shallots, chopped

3 garlic cloves, very finely chopped

1 large courgette, diced

1 pasilla chilli (a medium-hot dried chilli pepper), cored, deseeded and diced

½ red and ½ green pepper, cored, deseeded, diced

1 small head of broccoli, cut into small florets

½ bunch of asparagus, tough ends trimmed, cut into 2.5cm pieces on the bias

240ml low-salt chicken stock

1 bunch of kale, destemmed and chopped

Leaves from 3 sprigs of fresh thyme

For the batter

125g plain flour

1½ teaspoons chopped fresh rosemary

1 teaspoon baking powder

½ teaspoon each black pepper and sea salt

300ml full-fat milk

115g unsalted butter for the baking tin

85g Gruyère cheese, grated

1. Position an oven shelf in the centre and preheat the oven to 180°C/gas mark 4.

2. To make the vegetables, heat 2 tablespoons of the oil in a large frying pan over a medium-high heat. Add the potatoes, season with 1 teaspoon of the salt, the cayenne and dried thyme, reducing the heat a little, and sauté for about 5 minutes until the potatoes start to brown. Add the carrot and cook for 5 minutes until it is softened and the potatoes are cooked through. Remove the potatoes and carrots and set aside. Drizzle the remaining tablespoon of oil into the pan over a medium-high heat. Add the onion, season with ½ teaspoon salt and sauté for 5-7 minutes until tender and translucent. Sprinkle in the shallots and garlic and sauté for 1-2 minutes until the garlic is fragrant, stirring constantly so that it doesn't brown. Stir in the courgette, chilli, peppers, broccoli, asparagus and remaining 1 teaspoon salt and sauté for about 5 minutes to soften the vegetables. Add the chicken stock, kale and fresh thyme and bring to a simmer. Reduce the heat and simmer for about 5 minutes, or until the broth is thick enough to coat the back of a spoon. Turn off the heat. Using a slotted spoon, transfer 2 breakfast cupfuls of the sautéed vegetables to a bowl and set aside. Leave the vegetables remaining in the pan to cool slightly, then purée them with the broth left in the pan using a stick blender to make a gravy.

3. To make the batter, in a large bowl, mix together the flour, rosemary, baking powder, pepper and salt until thoroughly combined. Whisk in the milk.

4. Put the butter in a large (23 × 33cm or 23cm round) baking tin. Put the tin in the oven for about 3 minutes to melt the butter. Remove the pan from the oven. Pour the batter into the centre of the tin and allow it to spread out naturally to cover the base of the tin. Spoon the vegetable mixture into different places on the batter so that there is some batter visible in between clumps of vegetables. Bake on the centre shelf for 15-20 minutes until the batter is set and starts to brown. Remove the buckle from the oven and sprinkle the cheese over the top. Bake for a further 8-10 minutes until the cheese is melted and crisp in places. Serve with the vegetable gravy.

Broad Bean Pilaf

One of my favourite places to go when I'm on tour is Beirut. I absolutely love it, love it, love it. One of the reasons is the food. Out of all the Mediterranean cuisines, which in general are among my favourites, Lebanese food is just the best. I feel like Lebanese cuisine is the French cuisine of the Middle East. It is more refined than other foods of the region. The last time I was in Lebanon, I had a broad bean and rice dish that I fell in love with. Then I came across the same rice dish at a Middle Eastern restaurant in my neighbourhood in Los Angeles. After eating the rice dish a few times, I figured out how to make it at home. It's so simple. I love broad beans, but they have such a short, spring-summer season. Recipes like this one, that use dried broad beans, allow me to eat them when fresh aren't in season. You could make this with dried butter beans in place of broad beans.

SERVES 6-8

25g unsalted butter

2 tablespoons olive oil

225g dried fava (broad) beans, soaked overnight and drained

½ medium yellow onion, very finely chopped

2 teaspoons sea salt

¼ teaspoon black pepper

185g basmati rice, rinsed thoroughly

2 garlic cloves, very finely chopped

3 tablespoons chopped fresh dill

710ml low-salt chicken stock

1. Heat the butter and oil in a large frying pan over a high heat until the butter is melted. Add the fava beans and onion.

2. Season with 1 teaspoon of the salt and ⅛ teaspoon of the pepper and sauté for about 5 minutes until the onion is tender and translucent, stirring often so that the onion doesn't brown. Stir in the rice, garlic and dill and cook for about 2 minutes until the rice is translucent.

3. Pour the chicken stock into the pan and add the remaining 1 teaspoon salt and ⅛ teaspoon pepper. Bring the stock to the boil over a high heat. Reduce the heat, cover and simmer for about 15 minutes until the rice is cooked.

4. Turn off the heat and leave the pilaf to rest for 5 minutes, covered. Fluff up the pilaf with a fork and serve.

Farro Salad with Ginger Sesame Glaze

I eat a lot of grains. Long before the whole surge in popularity of foods like quinoa and kale, I was using quinoa, as well as other grains, including farro, bulgur wheat, and barley, to make pizza dough, mac and cheese, and salads – you name it. Farro is similar to barley. It has a chewy texture that I love. I started eating it when I was pregnant, but it's now a staple in my house. This salad has a really surprising combination of textures and flavours, including fresh ginger, diced apples and pancetta. If you want to get a head start preparing this salad, cook the farro and make the vinaigrette the day before you plan to serve.

INGREDIENT NOTE: Acidulated water is water mixed with acid used to prevent oxidation, such as the apples in this recipe, from browning. To make acidulated water, mix 1 teaspoon lemon juice or vinegar with 475ml water.

COOK'S TIP: Hot ingredients expand when they're puréed in a blender, so unless you take the right precautions, they will explode in your blender, making a big (and possibly dangerous!) mess. To avoid this, when blending hot liquids, let the mixture you are blending cool for at least 5 minutes before transferring it to a blender. Fill the blender no more than halfway, then put the lid on the blender, leaving one corner open. To be on the extra-safe side, you can cover the lid with a kitchen towel to catch any splatters before turning on the blender.

SERVES 4–6

830ml low-salt chicken stock

370g farro

1 Granny Smith apple, unpeeled, finely chopped and placed in a bowl of acidulated water (see Ingredient Note)

225g pancetta or streaky bacon, cut into 5mm cubes

130g frozen garden peas, defrosted in a colander

4 medium shallots, thinly sliced

2 garlic cloves, very finely chopped

1 pinch of cayenne pepper

Sea salt and black pepper

250g homemade Ginger Sesame Glaze (page 90) or my Bounty & Full Ginger Sesame Glaze (order it online at bounty-full.myshopify.com)

1. Bring the chicken stock to the boil in a medium saucepan over a high heat. Add the farro and return the stock to the boil. Reduce the heat, cover the pan and simmer for 25–30 minutes until the farro is al dente and all the liquid has been absorbed. Transfer the farro to a large bowl and set it aside to cool to room temperature.

2. Cook the pancetta in a sauté pan over a medium-high heat until it's crispy. Drain on kitchen paper and add the pancetta to the bowl with the farro.

3. Drain the apples and add them to the bowl with the farro and pancetta. Toss in the peas, shallots and garlic, sprinkle with the cayenne and season with salt and pepper. Drizzle with the Ginger Sesame Glaze and toss to combine the ingredients. Serve at room temperature.

Tomato Burrata Salad with Avocado Grapefruit Dressing

I love tomatoes and avocados, and use burrata, which is so creamy and wondrous, any time I can find a way. This isn't a lettuce-based salad. It's more in the Greek or Italian tradition, where they serve just cucumbers, or in this case, just tomatoes, and call it a salad. The dressing is made of puréed avocados so it's thick and creamy.

SERVES 4

For the vinaigrette dressing

1 avocado, halved, stoned and peeled

165ml orange juice

80ml extra virgin olive oil

120ml white balsamic vinegar

1 tablespoon chopped yellow onion

2 teaspoons grapefruit juice

1 teaspoon sea salt

1 teaspoon black pepper

2 garlic cloves, smashed

1 jalapeño pepper, roughly choppe

1½ tablespoons roughly chopped fr coriander

For the salad

3 large heirloom or vine-ripened tomatoes

1 ball of burrata, 200–250g, or 2 balls, 125g each, of mozzarella cheese

Sea salt and black pepper

35g raw unsalted pistachios

1. To make the vinaigrette, combine all of the ingredients in the jug of a blender and purée until smooth.

2. Cut the tomatoes into quarters and arrange them on a serving platter. Place the cheese in the centre of the platter and sprinkle the tomatoes and cheese with salt and pepper. Drizzle about 120ml of the dressing over the salad, scatter the pistachios over the top and serve. Leftover vinaigrette can be stored in the fridge in an airtight container for several days.

Yellow Beans with Fried Salt Pork

Sometimes, when I'm on tour, people bring me gifts, some of which make no sense at all, and others that totally make sense. When I was on tour for my album FOOD, I started getting a lot of food gifts, which was fun. People brought cupcakes, homemade crackers, jams, honeys. In San Francisco, this sweet guy – I think Rob was his name – brought me an entire gift basket of food. He lives in Napa, where he told me he has all kinds of friends with all these amazing markets and restaurants. He'd made me a really spectacular gift basket with items from the area: cookies, oils, vinegars, and a lot of really cool dried beans that I'd never seen before. I turned some of the beans into a soup (see Three Bean Soup with Ají, page 45). And I cooked a bag of yellow beans with cubes of fried salt pork and ate the beans as a side dish. They came out so hearty and so delicious. Even though I soaked them overnight, the dried beans took forever to cook. My husband loves to drizzle olive oil on these and every other kind of beans.

SERVES 4

Rapeseed or vegetable oil for deep-frying

115g salt belly pork or unsmoked streaky bacon in one piece, cut into 1cm cubes

450g light-coloured dried beans (or any dried bean will work), soaked overnight and drained

½ large Spanish onion, diced

6 garlic cloves, very finely chopped

2 large sprigs of fresh rosemary

1 sprig of fresh thyme

2 teaspoons sea salt, or to taste

1½ teaspoons black pepper

1 litre low-salt chicken stock, or as needed

1. Heat the oil in a small saucepan over a high heat until it reaches 180°C.

2. Add the salt pork and fry for 3–5 minutes until crisp. Using a slotted spoon, remove the pork from the oil and transfer it to a large saucepan.

3. To the saucepan, add the rest of the ingredients (except the chicken stock) and enough water to cover the beans by 2.5cm. Bring the water to the boil over a high heat.

4. Reduce the heat and simmer the beans for 1–1½ hours until tender and mushy, adding the stock gradually so that the beans are constantly covered with liquid throughout the cooking process. Check and adjust the seasoning if necessary.

Kale Salad
with Guava Vinaigrette

Kale this, kale that – kale is everywhere. I don't want to eat something just because it's good for me; it has to taste good, too. The crispiness of the kale with the sweet graininess of the guava is the perfect match.

INGREDIENT NOTE:
You can often find frozen guava purée sold in bags in grocery stores. If you can't locate it, use mango purée. And if you can't find that, buy frozen cubes of mango and purée them in a blender.

SERVES 4

For the vinaigrette

60ml grapeseed oil or extra-virgin olive oil

60ml puréed fresh or canned guava or mango (see Ingredient Note)

2 tablespoons white wine vinegar or champagne vinegar

2 tablespoons very finely chopped shallot (about 1 small shallot)

1 teaspoon Dijon mustard

¼ teaspoon sea salt

¼ teaspoon black pepper

⅛ teaspoon ground cumin

⅛ teaspoon cayenne pepper

For the salad

1 bunch of cavolo nero (aka black or Tuscan kale), leaves stacked, rolled and thinly sliced

½ medium heirloom tomato, diced

6 medium ready-to-eat dried apricots

about 14 caramelised pecan halves

¼ small red onion, thinly sliced

1. To make the vinaigrette, whisk together all of the ingredients in a small bowl.

2. In a large bowl, combine the kale, tomato, apricots, pecans and red onion slices. Drizzle with about 6 tablespoons of the vinaigrette and toss to combine, making sure you coat all of the salad ingredients with the vinaigrette. Add more dressing to taste, if you choose. Leftover vinaigrette can be stored in the fridge in an airtight container for several days.

Spinach Salad
with Manchego Cheese & Bloody Mary Vinaigrette

When I did a 31-day raw food diet, I got very creative with raw vegetables, salads in particular. I'm such a carnivore that it was definitely a challenge for me to eat as many vegetables as I did that month. In the process, I learned that if the salad contained different textures, especially something chewy and crunchy, it felt more satisfying. I love the texture of raw hazelnuts, so I threw them into a lot of my salads, along with dried fruits. This salad, which contains chopped hazelnuts and dried blueberries, became one of my go-to salads during that period, and one that I continue to make even when I'm not dieting. Of course, now I can add some cheese (wink).

SERVES 4

For the vinaigrette

300ml tequila

1 × 500g can passata

80ml sherry vinegar

50g preserved garlic cloves from a jar, very finely chopped

60ml juice from a jar of pepperoncini chilli peppers

35g very finely chopped red onion

6 garlic cloves, very finely chopped

2½ tablespoons black pepper

2 tablespoons fresh lime juice

2 tablespoons bottled hot sauce (I like sriracha or my own Bounty & Full Hot Sauce)

2 tablespoons prepared horseradish

1½ teaspoons smoked salt or sea salt

For the salad

250g pre-washed baby spinach

3 heirloom or vine-ripened tomatoes, chopped

1 yellow pepper, halved, deseeded and thinly sliced

1 portobello mushroom, cleaned and very thinly sliced

1 jalapeño pepper, trimmed and sliced into thin rounds

70g hazelnuts, chopped

35g celery, sliced

40g dried blueberries

110g Manchego, thinly sliced on a mandolin

1. To make the vinaigrette, bring the tequila to a simmer in a saucepan over a high heat and cook for 1 minute to burn off the alcohol. Set aside to cool slightly. Pour the tequila into a medium bowl and whisk in the remaining ingredients.

2. To make the salad, assemble all the ingredients except the cheese in a bowl. Drizzle with 120ml of vinaigrette and toss gently to coat and distribute the ingredients. Scatter the cheese slices over the top and serve.

Carrot & New Potato Rösti

After church on Sundays in New York, we used to go to Theresa's, a Polish place on the Lower East Side, for pierogi and blintzes. One of my favourite things were the latkes, or potato pancakes. Later in life, as a result of travelling and going to culinary school, I realised that many cultures make potato pancakes, they just call them by different names. I add carrot to mine; I like the colour and sweetness it adds – plus, I'm always trying to sneak vegetables into dishes to get my son to eat them. These make a nice brunch item. Although here I make one large rösti, you can make smaller ones in individual pans, which are not only cute, but easier to flip.

SERVES 4

2 Desiree potatoes, about 450g, and 1 large carrot, grated on the largest hole of a box grater

¼ large yellow onion, very finely chopped minced

4 garlic cloves, very finely chopped

2 tablespoons wholemeal flour

2 teaspoons sea salt

40g ghee or unsalted butter

1. In a large bowl, mix the grated potatoes and carrots with the onion, garlic, flour and salt.

2. Melt the ghee in a large sauté pan over a medium heat. Tip the rösti mixture into the pan and press gently with a spatula to form the rösti to the shape of the pan. Reduce the heat to medium-low and cook for about 10 minutes, continuing to press on the veggies until the potatoes are deep golden brown and crispy. Flip the rösti and cook the second side, then slide it out of the pan onto a plate, cut it into four wedges and serve hot.

Ginger Sesame Glaze

I've been making ginger sesame glaze forever. It goes with so many different things. I always have it in my fridge, and now that I have my own sauce line, I always have cases of the Bounty & Full Ginger Sesame Glaze for emergencies. I use it to make Ginger Sesame Glazed Shrimp with Pak Choi (page 134) and Farro Salad with Ginger Sesame Glaze (page 82). It's a great salad dressing.

MAKES ABOUT 300G

85g honey

2 tablespoons toasted sesame oil

2 tablespoons soy sauce

2 tablespoons rice wine vinegar

2 garlic cloves, roughly chopped

1 large yellow onion, roughly chopped

2.5cm piece of fresh ginger, peeled and roughly chopped

sea salt and black pepper, to taste

1. Combine all of the ingredients in a saucepan and bring to the boil over a high heat. Reduce the heat and simmer, stirring, until the garlic and onion are soft. Set aside for 5 minutes to cool. Transfer to the jug of a blender or the bowl of a mini food processor and blend to a smooth paste. Transfer any leftovers to a glass jar or airtight container and refrigerate for up to 7 days.

Mains

'I didn't really know
who I was until I started
cooking purposefully.
Look at all the people
who have travelled to
this country to call
it home.'

Drunken Fried Chicken

This recipe came about when I was researching Peking duck and Korean fried chicken. After learning everything I could about them, I decided to blend ideas and try making a fried chicken dish of my own creation. It took a lot of failed attempts to get to this, but I did it. The chicken is delicious.

COOK'S TIP: It's important to fry this chicken at a lower-than-normal temperature, otherwise the soy sauce will burn and taste bitter. Use a deep-frying thermometer to ensure the correct temperature.

SERVES 4

600ml soy sauce

240ml rice wine or sake

170g runny honey

10g fresh ginger, finely sliced

2 tablespoons black pepper

1 tablespoon garlic powder

1 whole chicken, cut into 10 pieces

160g potato flour

160g rice flour

Vegetable or corn oil for frying (I can't use it because I'm allergic, but groundnut oil would be an awesome option, too)

1. In a large bowl, whisk together the soy sauce, vinegar, honey, ginger, pepper and garlic powder. Add the chicken pieces to the bowl and turn to coat them with the marinade. Cover the bowl and refrigerate the chicken overnight or for at least 4 hours.

2. Heat 7.5–10cm of the oil in a large saucepan until it reaches 180°C.

3. Mix the potato and rice flours together in a large bowl. On the work surface, make a bed of kitchen paper. One by one, remove the chicken pieces from the marinade and put them on the kitchen paper to drain. Blot off any excess marinade and dredge the chicken in the flour mixture, then fry the chicken in the hot oil, about 8 minutes for smaller pieces and 12 minutes for larger pieces, turning now and then. The chicken will be a deep mahogany colour and the juices will run clear when pierced with a small knife. Transfer the chicken pieces to the kitchen paper to drain.

Orange Chilli Chicken

This is my 'natural' version of orange chicken from a Chinese restaurant. Serve with brown or white rice.

INGREDIENT NOTE: You can find chilli oil in the Asian condiment section of supermarkets. I use chilli oil a lot because it adds a really good, robust flavour to dishes along with its heat.

SERVES 4–6

For the sauce

4–5 navel oranges

2 tablespoons rapeseed or vegetable oil

2 tablespoons chilli oil (see Ingredient Note)

1½ yellow onions, chopped

2 teaspoons sea salt, plus more to taste

6 garlic cloves, thinly sliced

3–10 spicy chillies (such as red or green serrano or jalapeño peppers, Fresno chillies, red red bird's eye chillies or habanero chillies), finely chopped, including the seeds

1 litre low-salt chicken stock, plus more if reheating

¾ teaspoon smoked paprika

150g sugar

250g honey

For the chicken

Rapeseed or vegetable oil for deep-frying

900g skinless, boneless chicken breasts

2 teaspoons sea salt

2 teaspoons black pepper

1 teaspoon garlic granules

500g plain flour

3 medium eggs, lightly beaten

120g cornflour

1. To make the sauce, thinly slice 1 orange and set aside. Peel the second orange with a vegetable peeler and thinly slice the zest into julienne. Juice the peeled orange and the remaining oranges into a measuring jug to get 180ml juice and set aside.

2. Heat the rapeseed and chilli oils in a large sauté pan over a medium-high heat. Add the onions, 1 teaspoon of the salt and sauté, stirring often, for about 20 minutes until they are tender and caramelised (golden brown). Sprinkle in the garlic and chillies and sauté for about 2 minutes until the garlic is fragrant, stirring constantly so that it doesn't burn. Add the reserved orange slices, orange zest and the paprika. Stir in the sugar and the remaining 1 teaspoon salt and cook for about 2 minutes until the sugar dissolves and begins to bubble. Pour in the reserved orange juice and the chicken stock and bring the liquid to a simmer. Stir in the honey, reduce the heat and simmer for about 25 minutes until the sauce is the consistency of a glaze (it should be thick enough to coat the chicken).

3. While the sauce is cooking, prepare the chicken. Heat 7.5–10cm of oil in a large saucepan over a medium-high heat until it reaches 180°C. Create a bed of kitchen paper for draining. Cut the chicken into 4cm chunks and season with the salt, pepper and garlic granules.

4. Pour half of the flour into a medium bowl. Whisk the eggs in a second bowl and combine the remaining flour with the cornflour in a third bowl. Line the bowls up in this order: flour, egg, flour-cornstarch mixture. Dredge the chicken pieces in the flour, then the egg and then in the flour-cornstarch mixture. Put the finished pieces in a glass baking dish.

5. Working in batches and being careful not to overcrowd the pan, drop the chicken pieces in the oil and fry for about 5 minutes until golden brown and crisp. Transfer to the kitchen paper to drain. Cook the remaining chicken pieces in the same way, allowing the oil return to 180°C before adding the second batch of chicken.

6. If the glaze is cool, reheat it over a medium-low heat, adding more stock to thin it if necessary. Add the chicken pieces to the pan and toss to coat the chicken with the glaze.

Coconut Curry with Chicken & Vegetables

Many years ago, I stayed for a few months with a friend, Rodrigo Otazu, at his house in Bali, which is where I first encountered this curry dish. I like to think that, over the years, I've made it my own. In this recipe, I call for a whole chicken, cut up. Cooking the chicken on the bone gives the sauce such a good flavour. I also think it looks better, seeing meat on the bone rather than little cubes of meat in a sauce. Serve it with white rice or bulgur wheat tossed with golden raisins or black currants. The mix of coconut milk and bulgur makes you feel like you're doing something right for your body. This dish is delicious with lamb or prawns, too.

SERVES 4

1 whole chicken, cut into 10 pieces

2½ teaspoons sea salt, plus more to taste

1 teaspoon black pepper

1 teaspoon smoked paprika

3 tablespoons coconut oil

1½ large yellow onions, thinly sliced

1 green and 1 red pepper, cored, deseeded and thinly sliced

4 garlic cloves, thinly sliced

1 tablespoon peeled, grated fresh ginger

55g cup plus 1 tablespoon soft light or dark brown sugar

3 tablespoons curry powder (preferably hot)

3 carrots, thinly sliced into rounds

8 small salad potatoes, halved lengthways

3 × 400ml cans coconut milk, warmed over a low heat

60ml fresh lime juice

1 head of broccoli, cut into florets

Steamed white or brown rice for serving

1 recipe Mango Chutney (page 138)

1. Season the chicken with 2 teaspoons of the salt, ½ teaspoon of the pepper and ½ teaspoon of the paprika.

2. Heat the oil in a large sauté pan over a medium-high heat. Cook the chicken in the hot oil for about 5 minutes per side until browned on both sides. Remove the chicken from the pan and set aside.

3. Add the onions, red and green peppers, garlic and ginger to the pan, season with the remaining ½ teaspoon salt and sauté for 3–4 minutes until the vegetables begin to soften. Reduce the heat to medium, stir in the sugar and cook the vegetables with the sugar for 1–2 minutes until they are caramelised. Stir in the curry powder.

4. Add the carrots, potatoes, warmed coconut milk and lime juice and bring the liquid to a simmer. Reduce the heat to low and simmer the curry for 10 minutes to begin to thicken the sauce.

5. Return the chicken pieces to the pan and continue to simmer the curry until it is thick and creamy. Add the broccoli and cook for about 2 minutes until tender. Serve with the steamed rice and chutney.

Malay Curry Chicken

One year, I performed at a Formula One race in Kuala Lumpur. While I was there, I had some spare time, so I asked one of the chefs at the hotel where I was staying if he would teach me how to make really traditional Malay curry, which is served everywhere from outdoor markets to fine restaurants and hotels.

SERVES 4

1.1kg skinless chicken breast, thinly sliced

2½ teaspoons sea salt, plus more to taste

80ml red curry paste

1 teaspoon ground coriander

½ teaspoon ground cumin

½ teaspoon ground fennel seeds

¼ teaspoon ground cardamom

7.5cm piece of fresh ginger, peeled and roughly chopped

130g peeled shallots, roughly chopped

8 garlic cloves, roughly chopped

25g ghee (or use unsalted butter)

1 tablespoon tomato purée

240ml low-salt chicken stock

3 fresh curry leaves (see Ingredient Note, page 46)

2 star anise

1 cinnamon stick

250g natural Greek yogurt

1. Slice the chicken breasts into 1cm-thick pieces and season with 2 teaspoons of the salt. Set aside.

2. In a small bowl, combine the curry paste, coriander, cumin, fennel and cardamom with enough water to form a thick paste and set aside.

3. In the jug of a blender or the bowl of a mini food processor, combine the ginger, shallots, garlic and the remaining ½ teaspoon salt and purée to make a paste. Melt the ghee in a large sauté pan over a medium heat. Scrape in the contents of the blender or food processor and cook, stirring constantly, for about 2 minutes until the garlic is fragrant. Stir in the spice paste and tomato purée and cook for 3–5 minutes until slightly caramelised. Add the chicken stock, curry leaves, star anise and cinnamon stick and cook, scraping up the cooked bits from the base of the pan, for about 1 minute. Add the chicken and bring the stock to the boil. Reduce the heat and simmer for about 7 minutes just to cook the chicken through. Turn off the heat. Put the yogurt in a small bowl and gradually add 240ml of the curry sauce from the pan, whisking constantly. Stir the yogurt mixture back into the curry sauce and chicken and serve.

Duck Fried Quinoa

My mum is half Chinese, so in addition to Puerto Rican cuisine, I grew up eating a lot of Asian food. Although the quinoa in this dish would really piss her off (she always says, 'Quinoa this! Kale that! All these trendy ingredients!'), it was, in a sense, inspired by her, since she taught me to cook with a wok, and to make fried rice. It was also inspired by the meat and bones I had left after making and serving Peking Duck (page 103). If you have leftover duck bones, boil them to make a quick, small batch of duck stock and use that instead of water when you make the quinoa.

SERVES 4

340g quinoa, rinsed thoroughly

4 medium eggs

¼ teaspoon sea salt

25g unsalted butter

3 garlic cloves

4 tablespoons plus 1 teaspoon sesame oil

1cm piece of fresh ginger, peeled and thinly sliced

¼ large yellow onion, diced

½ carrot, diced

4 tablespoons soy sauce

125–250g shredded duck (you can substitute dark chicken meat)

3 spring onions, thinly sliced

70g frozen petit pois

25g beansprouts

1. Bring 480ml water to the boil in a small saucepan over a high heat. Add the quinoa and return the water to the boil. Reduce the heat to low, cover the pan and cook until the quinoa is tender and the water is evaporated. Turn off the heat and set aside to rest, covered, for at least 5 minutes.

2. Beat the eggs with the salt. Heat the butter in a large sauté pan (preferably non-stick) over a medium heat. Pour in the egg mixture and gently scramble the eggs for 2–3 minutes, taking care not to overcook them.

3. Very finely chop 2½ of the garlic cloves and set aside, reserving the remaining half. Heat a wok over a high heat. Add the 1 teaspoon sesame oil, along with 1 slice of the ginger and the half garlic clove, using a fork or spatula to drag the ginger and garlic around the wok 4 or 5 times.

4. Add another tablespoon of the sesame oil and allow it to heat for 1 minute. Sauté the onion in the sesame oil for 5 minutes until softened, stirring often so that it doesn't brown.

5. Add the chopped garlic and sauté for 1–2 minutes, stirring constantly so that it doesn't brown. Add the carrot and the remaining sliced ginger and sauté for 2–3 minutes to soften.

6. Add 1 tablespoon of the sesame oil and 1 tablespoon of the soy sauce and then stir in the duck, quinoa and scrambled eggs.

7. Add the remaining 2 tablespoons of oil and 3 tablespoons of soy sauce to the wok, along with the spring onions, peas and beansprouts and cook for 1–2 minutes to warm the vegetables through.

Crispy Peking Duck

I love duck; it's my favourite of the poultry groups, because it's all dark meat. I've made duck many different ways, but it was fairly recently that I tried making Peking duck for the first time. Peking duck requires a few steps, and you have to plan a few days ahead, but it's worth the effort. The key is to dry out the skin, so that when it cooks, it gets nice and crispy. To do this, you separate the skin from the flesh. The traditional way is to take a straw, stick it between the skin and flesh, and blow to get air under the skin. I tried but it didn't work for me. I almost gave myself a hernia and the skin didn't separate. Instead, I did it with a wooden spoon.

INGREDIENT NOTE: I use Malta, a malt-based non-alcoholic beverage popular in some Hispanic and South American cultures, to glaze the skin. If you can't find it, use soy sauce instead.

SERVES 4–6

2 tablespoons plus 1½ teaspoons sea salt

2 teaspoons baking powder

1 whole duck, weighing 1.8–2kg

2 tablespoons soy sauce or 120ml Malta (see Ingredient Note)

170g runny honey

2 jasmine tea bags

1. Combine 2 tablespoons of the salt and the baking powder in a small bowl. Put a roasting rack inside a baking tray.

2. Pat the duck dry with kitchen paper. Using your hands, carefully separate the duck's skin from the meat, starting at the bottom of the breast and working upwards, taking care to keep the skin attached to the duck and also not to tear the skin. Rub the salt and baking powder mixture over the skin of the duck and place the duck on the roasting rack set in the baking tray. Refrigerate the duck, uncovered, for 2–3 days until the skin is dry and leathery looking.

3. Position an oven shelf as close to the bottom of the oven as possible and remove any shelves above it to make room for the duck. Preheat the oven to 180°C/gas mark 4.

4. Transfer the duck on its roasting rack from the fridge to the sink. Fill a pan large enough to hold the duck with water and bring the water to the boil over a high heat. Dump half the boiling water over the duck. Turn the duck over and dump the other half of the boiling water on the second side. Set the duck aside on the roasting rack with the baking tray underneath to dry for at least 5 minutes.

5. In a small bowl, combine the Malta (or soy sauce) and honey with the remaining 1½ teaspoons salt and brush the glaze over the surface of the duck. Put the tea bags inside the cavity of the duck. Fill an empty can (such as a beer can) with water and put it in the cavity of the duck so that you will be able to set it upright.

6. Set up the baking tray with the roasting rack in it as you did before. Break or remove the duck's tail to get the duck to stand upright. Roast for 1 hour, rotating it from front to back midway through the roasting time so that it browns evenly, until it is a deep mahogany colour. Reduce the heat to 120°C/gas mark ½ and continue roasting for about 30 minutes until fat stops dripping from the cavity. Set the duck aside to rest for 10 minutes before carving. If the duck has shrunken around the can, using kitchen scissors, cut down the back of the spine so the meat naturally falls from the bone. Don't cut too deep as the can is still inside the bird. Remove the can carefully to not spill the excess water that remains in the can onto the duck.

Turkey Meatloaf with Ground Walnuts

Meatloaf is totally American. It's hearty. It's simple. And I love it. You can do a million different things when making meatloaf. Beef meatloaf is the most traditional, but in recent years, turkey meatloaf has come a close second in popularity. It's so easy to make, and you can serve it for dinner, then have leftover meatloaf in sandwiches the next day. I like to serve this meatloaf with the Wholegrain and Veggie Buckle (page 79) so I can spoon the veggie gravy made from the buckle over the meatloaf.

SERVES 6-8

900g turkey mince

3 medium carrots, roughly chopped

½ yellow onion

½ green pepper, cored, deseeded and roughly chopped

2 medium eggs, lightly beaten

280g walnuts, coarsely ground in a food processor

4 garlic cloves, smashed and roughly chopped

1½ tablespoons mustard powder

1 tablespoon sea salt

1 tablespoon fresh thyme leaves

3 tablespoons smoked paprika

1 teaspoon black pepper

1. Position one oven shelf in the centre and preheat the oven to 180°C/gas mark 4. Set aside the turkey in a large bowl.

2. In the bowl of a food processor with the metal blade, process the carrots, onion and green pepper until very finely chopped. Transfer the vegetables to the bowl with the turkey. Add the eggs and half of the ground walnuts along with the garlic, mustard, salt, thyme, paprika and pepper and mix with your hands until thoroughly incorporated. Shape the meatloaf mixture into a football-shaped loaf with your hands. Coat the meatloaf with the remaining walnuts and put the loaf on a baking tray.

3. Bake the meatloaf on the middle shelf for about 1 hour, or until the centre of the meatloaf registers 71°C on an instant-read thermometer. Leave to cool slightly before slicing and serving.

Herb-Larded Turkey

Larding sounds intense, but it's really just injecting or adding fat and flavour to the meat. It gives the turkey a beautiful colour and the larding helps keep the turkey moist and flavourful, as well as enhancing the juices left in the pan. The turkey is delicious in sandwiches with Mandarin Orange Cranberry Sauce.

I celebrate Thanksgiving in the sense that I cook. I like that it is an American day for family, and for people to get together and just share a moment. I live in California, but I'm not from here, and I have a lot of friends who live here who are not from here. So I usually take in all the people who don't have family around either, and it feels like home. It's a day to eat and get together.

Ingredient note: Achiote or Annatto (*Bixa orellana*) is a Brazilian tree. The seeds are used in cooking, bringing a nice golden colour to the turkey here; the flavour is bitter and you just want to use a small amount of seeds, ground to a powder.

SERVES 8–10

1 whole turkey, weighing 5.4–6.3kg

1 bunch of fresh rosemary, leaves finely chopped, plus extra for the cavity

1 bunch of fresh thyme, leaves finely chopped, plus extra for the cavity

180g Sazón (page 21) or achiote paste, crumbled with your fingers

1 tablespoon smoked paprika

8 garlic cloves, smashed

1 tablespoon coarse ground pepper

2 tablespoons sea salt

120ml olive oil

170g unsalted butter, softened at room temperature

2 yellow onions, quartered

2 green peppers, halved and deseeded

1 recipe Mandarin Orange Cranberry Sauce (page 138)

1. Adjust the oven shelf to the lowest position and remove other shelves if necessary. Preheat the oven to 160°C/gas mark 3.

2. Pat the turkey dry thoroughly with kitchen paper. Set the bird aside to come to room temperature.

3. In a small bowl, combine the rosemary, thyme, achiote, paprika, garlic, pepper, salt, oil and butter, mashing the seasonings with the butter and oil to create a rub. Work the rub under the skin of the turkey and massage it into the breasts, legs and cavity. Massage the rub on the outside of the skin as well. Stuff the turkey cavity with the quartered onions, peppers and extra herbs. Tie the legs together over the back of breast with kitchen string and tuck in the ends of the wings so that they will be protected during cooking.

4. Roast the turkey for 1 hour. Reduce the heat to 150°C/gas mark 2 and roast for a further 1 hour 40 minutes, or until a thermometer inserted into the thickest part of the thigh registers 74°C. Remove the turkey from the oven, transfer to a large platter, cover loosely with foil and leave to rest 30 minutes before carving. Serve with the cranberry sauce on the side.

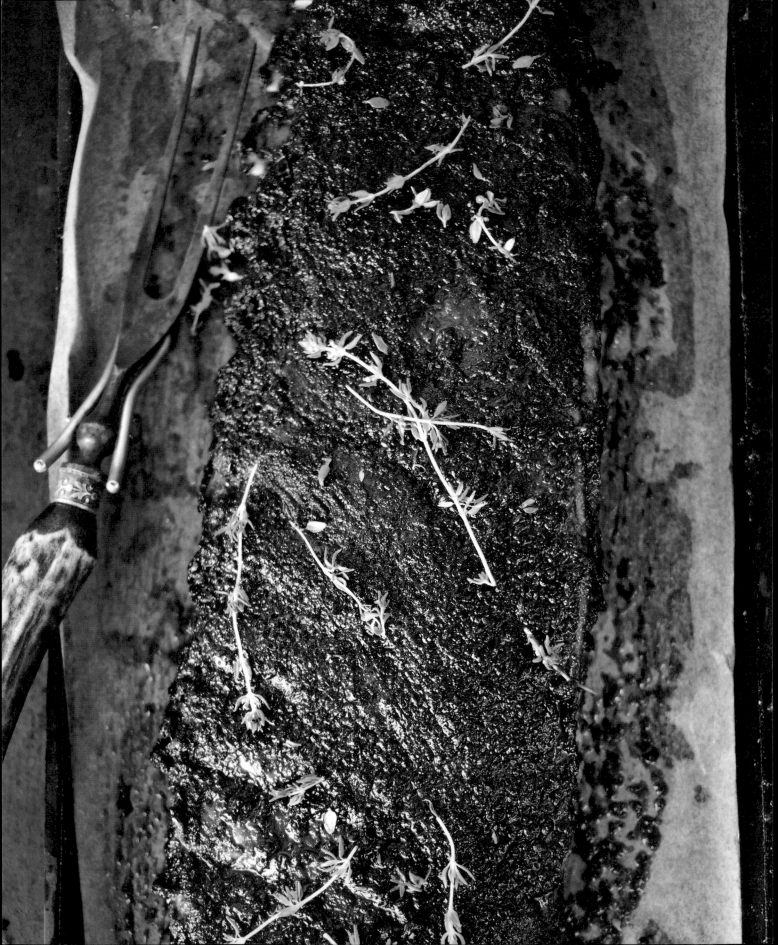

Jerk Ribs
with Brown Sugar Rub

When I moved to LA, I really found myself craving Jamaican food. In Harlem, it's readily available, but here, sadly, there just wasn't a good Jamaican restaurant. Even when friends suggested them, I'd go and try, and think, 'This is not good… actually, this is bad.' I like food from places with warm climates; like the people, the flavours are bold and loud, full of spice. They use a lot of flavours, colours and spices, and I just have an affinity with them. One day, I was especially craving Jamaican jerk, a seasoning blend that includes allspice, garlic, thyme, and other spices – every version is a bit different. I'd given up on finding decent Jamaican food in LA, so I experimented to make my own. Jerk is normally used with chicken but, since I'm a huge rib lover, I tried the same idea with ribs! First I rubbed them with a spicy brown sugar mix, then I coated them in sauce made with soy sauce, toasted sesame oil, garlic, thyme, molasses, and allspice. I brought the ribs to the studio one day when I was recording my last album. The whole band went wild over them. It's all we could talk about all afternoon, so I named the song we were working on that day 'Jerk Ribs'. It was the first single released off that album. The ribs are great. The song is pretty awesome too.

The Brown Sugar Rub is just delicious; you can put it on bacon, steak or lamb chops.

INGREDIENT NOTE: You might be surprised that I ask you to add the entire thyme sprigs, stems and all, to the blender when making the sauce. The stems are actually where the most flavour is in the herb and where most of the oils are, and when they're all blended up, they give the sauce its body.

SERVES 4

For the ribs

2 racks of pork ribs, 900g-1.3kg each

1 tablespoon sea salt

100g Spicy Brown Sugar Rub (see opposite)

1 teaspoon smoked paprika

For the sauce

120ml toasted sesame oil

85g molasses

2 tablespoons soy sauce

2 teaspoons ground allspice

4-6 garlic cloves, peeled

1-2 Scotch bonnet or habanero chillies, deseeded or whole (using the seeds will make the sauce very spicy)

1 bunch of spring onions, trimmed and roughly chopped

1 bunch of fresh sprigs of thyme (see Ingredient Note)

½ teaspoon black pepper

1. Position an oven shelf in the centre and preheat the oven to 200°C/gas mark 6.

2. Season both sides of the ribs with the salt. Stir the smoked paprika into the spice rub and coat both sides of the ribs with the rub. Place the ribs, bone side down, in a large baking dish. Cover the dish tightly with foil and roast the ribs on the centre shelf for 2-2¼ hours, rotating the baking dish from the top to the bottom shelves halfway through so that they cook evenly. The ribs are done when the meat separates easily from the bone.

3. While the ribs roast, make the jerk sauce. Combine all of the ingredients in the jug of a blender or the bowl of a food processor fitted with a metal blade and purée until smooth. Transfer the jerk mixture to a saucepan and bring it to the boil over a high heat. Reduce the

heat and simmer the sauce for 10–15 minutes until it darkens in colour.

4. Remove the ribs from the oven, but do not turn it off. Remove the foil but don't discard it. Using a basting brush or the back of a spoon, coat the ribs evenly with the jerk sauce. Cover the baking dish with the foil again and roast the ribs for a further 15 minutes. Serve the ribs with the rest of the sauce on the side.

Brown Sugar Rub

This rub is delicious – it has just enough caraway to offset the sweetness. I make it in big batches, so I always have some to hand, and use it to rub on stewed chicken, lamb chops, or steak. It just makes everything taste great. If you sprinkle it on bacon before cooking, it will change your life. The rub is light on salt because I like to salt meat directly and then add the rub, and this way I don't accidentally over-salt. Caraway, like cumin or nutmeg, is one of those seasonings that you have to be very sparing with. A little tastes amazing, but go too far and it'll overpower whatever you're making. When I'm cooking with these spices, I start by smelling the spice to remind myself how strong it is every time. Our sense of smell is a great measuring tool. Balance is key.

MAKES ABOUT 150G

220g soft light or dark brown sugar

2 tablespoons whole caraway seeds

2 tablespoons garlic granules

2 tablespoons sea salt

2 teaspoons cayenne pepper

1. Mix all of the ingredients together in a medium bowl. Use immediately or store in an airtight container at room temperature for up to several months.

Pernil:
Puerto Rican Pork Shoulder

Pernil is my favourite thing in the world. My grandmother made it. My mum made it. And now I make it. Make sure you get a pork shoulder with the skin on and bone in. When you slice into the roast, you see the gorgeous olives and garlic in every slice. I call for a 2.7–3.6kg roast, but make any size pernil you want; I like to have leftovers for sandwiches. It's hard to find large roasts sometimes, so order from your butcher ahead of time. My butcher orders it for me every other month and texts me when it comes in. Reserve the juices to make Arroz con Gandules (page 72).

SERVES 10-12

For the rub

170g unsalted butter, softened

180g achiote paste or Sazón (page 21)

120ml olive oil

2 tablespoons sea salt

1 tablespoon freshly coarsely ground black pepper

1 tablespoon very finely chopped fresh rosemary

1 tablespoon very finely chopped fresh thyme

1 tablespoon smoked paprika

1 tablespoon onion powder

1 tablespoon dried oregano

1 tablespoon ground cumin

For the pork

1 bone-in, skin-on pork shoulder weighing about 2.7–3.6kg

135g whole small pimento-stuffed olives

6 garlic cloves, smashed

480ml low-salt chicken stock or water, or as needed

1. To make the rub, combine the butter with the achiote paste, oil, salt, pepper, rosemary, thyme, paprika, onion powder, oregano and cumin, mashing the seasonings into the butter to make a paste.

2. To prepare the pork, rinse the pork shoulder under cold running water and pat it dry with kitchen paper. With a large sharp knife, stab the pork all over the surface, including the top, bottom and sides, penetrating about 5cm into the flesh. Using your hands, rub the paste all over the pork shoulder, working the mixture into the slits and under the skin. Insert the olives and garlic into the slits. Place the pork, skin side up, in a large roasting tin, cover with clingfilm and leave to marinate in the fridge for a minimum of 3 hours or up to 2 days.

3. When you're ready to roast the pork shoulder, adjust an oven shelf to the lowest position, removing other shelves if necessary. Preheat the oven to 200°C/gas mark 6.

4. Remove the pork from the fridge and leave to sit for 30 minutes to bring it to room temperature. Pour enough chicken stock into the pan to come about 2.5cm up the sides of the pork. Cover the tin tightly with foil and braise the pork for 3 hours, or until the meat is tender. Remove the pork from the oven. Remove and discard the foil, and return the pork to the oven to roast, uncovered, for 1 hour, or until the skin is dark brown and crisp. Set the pork aside to rest for at least 10 minutes before serving. Reserve the juices to make Arroz con Gandules (page 72). Slice the pork and serve.

Chicharrón

Chicharrón refers to fried pork belly; it's very common in Latino cooking. Slice it and eat it as a main dish with rice or mango, manchengo, beans or polenta, or use it to make sandwiches. Ask your butcher for a whole pork belly with the skin on. Slice it and spoon Ají (page 45) on it. It's fatty, meaty and wonderful.

SERVES 4

1 whole skin-on pork belly, weighing 700–900g

3 tablespoons sea salt

1 tablespoon black pepper

2 tablespoons garlic powder

2 tablespoons onion powder

Rapeseed or vegetable oil for deep-frying

1. Pour 2.8 litres of water into a baking dish large enough to hold the pork in a single layer. Stir in the salt, pepper, garlic and onion powders. Put the pork belly in the brine, cover and refrigerate for 3 days. Turn the pork daily.

2. Remove the pork belly from the brine and pat it with kitchen paper to dry. Make a bed of kitchen paper for draining.

3. Heat 10cm of oil in a large saucepan over a medium heat until it reaches 180°C. Gently slide the pork belly into the oil and fry for 20–30 minutes until the skin is hard and crackling to the touch. Remove the pork from the oil and set it, skin side up, on the kitchen paper to drain the oil and cool it slightly. Slice the chicharrón and use it to make a sandwich, or serve it with beans or cut it into cubes and snack on it.

Tostones

Known as Patacones in Colombian cuisine, I grew up on these and my husband also loves them. They are common in all Latin American countries. It's like a perfect marriage: chicharrón and tostones.

SERVES 4

Olive oil for deep frying

4 plantains, peeled

1 lemon, juiced

Sea salt

1. Heat the oil over a high heat in a medium size frying pan. Cut the plantains in half lengthways, lay them into the oil and fry for 3–4 minutes – they need to be just coloured and not cooked through.

2. Remove the plantains and pat dry on kitchen paper to remove excess oil.

3. Place them on a board and smash each half plantain with another board. Lay them on a clean piece of kitchen paper and evenly coat them with freshly squeezed lemon juice.

4. Reheat the oil, add the plantains and re-fry for 4–5 minutes until cooked all the way through. Remove the plantains with a slotted spoon and salt immediately. They should be golden and crispy.

Burrata-Stuffed Meatballs
with Pistachio Basil Pesto

I was a judge on Top Chef Masters one year, and one of my favourite dishes was a stuffed meatball. I borrowed that idea for these meatballs, which are stuffed with burrata (cream-filled mozzarella), and tossed with a beautiful, bright green pistachio pesto. I use a combination of beef, veal and pork. It's the traditional Italian way. I use leftover meatballs and pesto to make sandwiches.

COOK'S TIP: I have a little miniature food processor that I use exclusively for mincing garlic when I need more than just one or two cloves, such as for this recipe.

MAKES ABOUT 24 MEATBALLS; SERVES 6–8

450g pork mince

450g beef mince

450g veal mince

½ red onion, very finely chopped

6 garlic cloves, very finely chopped

1 tablespoon dried oregano

1 tablespoon plus 2 teaspoons sea salt

1 tablespoon smoked paprika

2 teaspoons dried basil

1 teaspoon black pepper

225g burrata

60g fresh breadcrumbs

2 tablespoons olive oil

1 recipe Pistachio Basil Pesto (page 139),
  at room temperature

1. In a large bowl, mix together the pork, beef, veal, red onion, garlic, oregano, salt, smoked paprika, basil and pepper, massaging the mixture with your hands to incorporate the ingredients without smashing the meat too much. Put the breadcrumbs on a plate. To shape the meatballs, take 70g of the meat and gently form a patty. Scoop a scant teaspoon of burrata into the centre, fold up the edges and gently roll the meat into a ball. Roll the balls in the breadcrumbs and put them on a baking tray. Repeat with the remaining meat mixture. For perfectly round meatballs, put the meatballs in the fridge for at least 1 hour and up to overnight to chill; chilling helps the meatballs hold their shape when cooked.

2. Heat the oil over a medium heat in a large sauté pan with a lid. Gently tap the excess breadcrumbs from the meatballs, add the meatballs to the oil and cook for 6–8 minutes until browned on all sides. Cover the pan, turn off the heat and leave for about 8 minutes until the meatballs are cooked all the way through from the residual heat in the pan. Remove the lid, pour the pesto over the meatballs and turn them gently to coat with the pesto. Serve immediately.

Swedish Meatballs

I've worked in Sweden a lot. I love Stockholm, and I love Swedish meatballs. I can't normally eat the same thing every day, but since meatballs are just about the only Swedish food I like, when I'm there I eat meatballs, mashed potatoes, and lingonberries every day. The meatballs have a slight sweetness to them, and great texture, and anything with a brown, creamy gravy is great. Most people I know have only had Swedish meatballs from IKEA. They're not bad, actually, for a frozen product, but they're nothing compared with the real thing. Naturally, I had to learn to make my own.

MAKES ABOUT 48 MEATBALLS; SERVES 6-8

For the meatballs

2 slices wholemeal or white bread

120ml full-fat milk

75g unsalted butter

½ large yellow onion, very finely chopped

2½ teaspoons sea salt

450g pork mince

450g beef mince

2 medium eggs, lightly beaten

1 teaspoon ground nutmeg

1 teaspoon ground allspice

For the gravy

115g unsalted butter

2 tablespoons plain flour

480ml beef stock

320ml double cream

1. Preheat the oven to 110°C/gas mark ¼.

2. To make the meatballs, cut the crusts off the bread and tear the bread into small pieces into a bowl. Pour the milk over the bread and set aside.

3. Melt 15g of the butter in a medium sauté pan over a medium heat. Add the onion, season with ½ teaspoon of the salt and sauté, stirring often, for about 12 minutes until the onion is soft and lightly browned. Add the onion to the bowl with the bread.

4. In a large bowl, mix together the minced meats, remaining 2 teaspoons salt and the nutmeg and allspice, incorporating the seasonings into the meats with your hands. Add the bread mixture and the eggs to the bowl and massage the ingredients together with your hands to combine.

5. Form the meat mixture into bite-sized balls (about 25g each) and place them on a baking tray. For perfectly round meatballs, put the meatballs in the fridge for at least 1 hour and up to overnight to chill; this will help the meatballs hold their shape when cooked.

6. Warm 30g of the remaining butter in a large sauté pan over a medium-high heat until it bubbles but doesn't brown. Add half of the meatballs and fry them for about 10 minutes until they are brown all over and cooked through. Transfer the meatballs to the baking tray or a heatproof plate and put them in the oven to keep warm while you fry the rest of the meatballs. Heat the remaining 30g butter and brown the remaining meatballs in the same way. Put the second batch of meatballs in the oven with the first batch.

7. To make the gravy, wipe out the pan you cooked the meatballs in. Melt the butter in the pan over a medium-low heat. Add the flour and cook, stirring with a whisk, for about 2 minutes until the flour is lightly browned. Gradually pour in the beef stock, stirring constantly with the whisk, and cook for about 10 minutes until the gravy begins to thicken. Stir in the cream and cook for about 2 minutes until the gravy is thick enough to coat the back of a spoon. Remove the meatballs from the oven and add them to the pan with the gravy. Turn to coat the meatballs on all sides with the gravy and serve.

Oxtail & Wild Mushroom Ragù

Italian food is so much more than tomato sauce, pasta, pizza, that kind of thing. What Italian food is, really, changes depending on where you are. When I was in Naples, I had a lot of stewed oxtails. They were very different from the oxtails I ate growing up (see Oxtail Stew, page 35), but they were delicious, and they were the inspiration for this ragù.

SERVES 6

1 recipe Fresh Spinach Pasta (page 125)

Semolina flour for dusting

15g unsalted butter

¼ yellow onion, cut into small dice

1 celery stick, cut into small dice

1 carrot, cut into small dice

1 teaspoon sea salt, plus more to taste

¼ teaspoon black pepper

700g wild mushrooms (such as chanterelle, shiitake or porcini), thinly sliced

125g shredded oxtail meat and 120ml gravy, reserved from Oxtail Stew (page 25)

250g Arrabiata Sauce (page 124)

Wedge of Parmesan cheese for grating

1. Roll out the pasta dough with a rolling pin, then pass it through a pasta machine and cut it into fettuccine. Transfer the pasta to a baking tray and sprinkle with semolina flour to prevent the strands from clumping together. Cover and refrigerate the pasta until you're ready to cook it, or for up to 3 days.

2. Melt the butter in a large frying pan over a medium heat. Add the onion, celery and carrot, sprinkle lightly with the salt and pepper and sauté for about 5 minutes until the vegetables have softened. Add the mushrooms and cook for about 10 minutes until they darken slightly and look heavy with the pan juices. Stir in the oxtail meat and juice along with the arrabiata sauce and cook for 3–5 minutes, stirring to distribute the meat and warm the sauce through. Season with more salt to taste. Set aside while you cook the pasta.

3. Bring a large pan of water to the boil and add enough salt so that it tastes like the ocean. Drop the pasta in the boiling water, stir so that it doesn't stick together and cook for 45 seconds. Drain the pasta and add it to the frying pan with the ragù. Toss to coat the pasta with the sauce. Transfer the pasta to serving plates and grate Parmesan over the top. Serve immediately.

Pineapple Beef

When I was about 15 years old, I worked near a restaurant on the Upper West Side in Manhattan called Penang. My two favourite dishes there were prawns with mango and beef with pineapple. It was my first encounter with Malaysian food, and it would be a long time before I realised that Penang was a place. Malaysia was a far-off land to me. I couldn't fathom what it would be like to be there. Fast forward just two years: I signed my first deal and, before I knew it, I was in Penang. I couldn't believe I was actually there! I loved the food at Penang the restaurant and in Penang the city, but it also became a symbol for me of how far I'd come. Before I ever had a career, before I knew what I was going to do with my life, I used to go to this restaurant for lunch and eat pineapple beef, and now here I was sitting on a beach in this really exotic, beautiful country. I felt in awe of life and how things can turn out. This dish, and that trip, have stayed with me all these years. Since then I've been able to travel to that part of the world extensively and there are so many luscious treasures to taste.

SERVES 4–6

3 rib-eye steaks, frozen and sliced 5mm thick

2½ teaspoons sea salt

3 teaspoons black pepper

25g unsalted butter or ghee

1 tablespoon chilli oil

½ large yellow onion, roughly chopped

1 pineapple, peeled, cored and cut into 2.5cm chunks

1 green pepper, cored, deseeded and roughly chopped

1 tablespoon peeled, finely grated fresh ginger

3 garlic cloves, very finely chopped

1½ teaspoons ground cumin

1 teaspoon curry powder

120ml pineapple juice

3 tablespoons soy sauce

2 tablespoons demerara sugar

225g sugar snap peas or mangetout, strings removed

4 spring onions, thinly sliced on the bias (white and green parts)

10g fresh coriander, chopped

Steamed white or brown rice for serving

1. Season the steaks with 2 teaspoons of the salt and 1 teaspoon of the pepper and set aside.

2. Melt the butter with the chilli oil in a large sauté pan over a medium-high heat. Add the onion, season with the remaining ½ teaspoon salt and sauté, stirring often, for about 5 minutes until it begins to soften. Toss in the pineapple, green pepper, ginger, garlic, cumin and curry powder and cook for about 5 minutes until the pepper softens. Stir in the pineapple juice, soy sauce and sugar. Bring to a simmer and cook for about 2 minutes to thicken the sauce. Increase the heat to high, add the steak and cook for about 1 minute. Stir in the peas and spring onions and cook for about 2 minutes to warm them through and take off the raw edge. Turn off the heat and stir in the coriander. Serve with white or brown rice.

Pastelón with Sweetcorn Béchamel

Pastelón, which is a layered casserole of platanos and picadillo (ground meat mixture), is a traditional casserole in Puerto Rican and Dominican cooking. You won't find it in a restaurant. It's something that you'll have at someone's house – their mother will make it, and you can never tell her that it isn't right, as she'll say her grandmother gave her the recipe. There's no right and wrong here! I use a combination of green plantains, which taste a bit like potatoes, and yellow, ripe plantains, which are sweet. I serve it with Sweetcorn Béchamel because I think everything needs sauce and it plays to the sweetness of the ripe plantains and the saltiness of the olives. Pastelón is a bit tedious to make, but you make a big casserole dish of it and it'll last you for a few days. I add chorizo to the meat mixture; I got the idea after my mum told me about a dish of plantains stuffed with chorizo. The contrast between the sweet plantains and the spicy chorizo is amazing. The best way to describe Pastelon is like a Puerto Rican lasagne or cusende, for lack of a better description. It's not something you've tried in festivals, it's something your mother would make – everyone makes it different. As I said, everyone makes it differently. Here's how I do it.

SERVES 6-8

6-8 plantains, half of them yellow, half green

Sea salt for the boiling water

Vegetable or vegetable oil for deep-frying

2 tablespoons olive oil

½ large Spanish onion, very finely chopped

¾ teaspoon black pepper

1 Anaheim chilli (California green chilli or chile verde), seeds and membrane removed, very finely chopped

450g beef mince

450g soft cooking chorizo, meat removed from the skins

1 tablespoon saffron threads

2 teaspoons Sazón (page 21) or ¼ teaspoon achiote paste, crumbled with your fingers

1 teaspoon finely chopped fresh oregano

½ teaspoon ground cumin

3 tablespoons roughly chopped green pimento-stuffed olives

110g hard cured chorizo, diced

Butter for greasing the baking dish

6 medium egg yolks

360ml whipping cream

150g extra-mature Cheddar cheese, grated

1 recipe Sweet Corn Béchamel (page 123)

1. Score the skins of the yellow and green plantains lengthways and remove and discard the skins. Slice 3-5mm thick lengthways, keeping the yellow and green separate.

2. Lay the green plantain slices flat in the base of a large pan and fill it with water. Make a bed of kitchen paper for draining. Bring the water to the boil over a high heat, salt it to taste like the ocean and boil the

plantains for about 30 minutes until tender. Drain the plantains and put them on the kitchen paper to dry.

3. Heat 5cm of the rapeseed oil in a large, straight-sided sauté pan over a medium-high heat until it reaches 180°C. On the work surface, make a bed of kitchen paper. Slide the yellow plantains into the oil and fry for 8–10 minutes until they are golden brown but still soft inside. Transfer to the kitchen paper to drain.

4. Heat the olive oil in large frying pan (preferably cast iron) over a medium heat. Add the onion, season with ¼ teaspoon of the pepper and cook, stirring often, for about 10 minutes until tender and translucent. Add the chilli, mince, cooking chorizo, saffron, achiote, oregano and cumin and cook for about 5 minutes until the meat is cooked through, breaking it up with a wooden spoon. Stir in the hard chorizo and olives. Turn off the heat and strain the fat from the meat, spooning out the oil with a large spoon or using kitchen paper to soak it up. Set aside while you prepare the other components of the casserole.

5. Grease the base and sides of a large baking dish with butter. Lay the plantain slices in the dish in a single layer as you would noodles for lasagne, alternating between green and yellow. Spread one-third of the meat mixture over the plantains. Lay down another layer of the plantains and another layer of meat until you have built three layers and used all of the plantains and meat.

6. Whisk the egg yolks, cream and remaining ½ teaspoon pepper together in a small bowl or glass measuring jug and pour evenly over the casserole. Scatter the cheese over the top. Bake the pastelón for 20–25 minutes until the cheese bubbles and browns and the egg is set. Set the pastelón aside to cool for 5–10 minutes before serving. Serve hot, cut into squares, with the béchamel on the side.

Sweetcorn Béchamel

Béchamel is one of the mother sauces in French cooking. I learnt to make it in culinary school, but who says we have to stick to the rules? When I make béchamel to serve with pastelónes, I add corn; I like the textural component and the burst of sweet flavour.

MAKES ABOUT 1KG

60g unsalted butter

3 medium shallots, very finely chopped

1 teaspoon sea salt, plus more to taste

30g plain flour

710ml full-fat milk

135g fresh or frozen sweetcorn kernels

1. Melt the butter in a medium saucepan over a low heat, but make sure that it doesn't brown. Add the shallots with 1 teaspoon of the salt, stirring often so that the shallots don't brown, for 4–5 minutes until they are tender and translucent.

2. Stir in the flour, whisking until no lumps remain. Cook, stirring constantly, for about 3 minutes until the flour is very light golden.

3. Gradually add 240ml of the milk, whisking until incorporated. Pour in the remaining milk and a good pinch of salt and bring the milk to the boil. Reduce the heat and simmer, stirring with a rubber spatula so that the sauce doesn't scorch on the base of the pan, until it is thick enough to coat the back of the spatula.

4. Stir in the corn and cook for about 2 minutes to warm it through. Add more salt to taste.

Fresh Spinach Pasta with Arrabiata Sauce

The process of making pasta to me feels like a love thing. It's not a quick fix. You start in the morning and you take a day to make it. Once I make the dough, I'll keep a boule of it in my freezer. I feel like if you're going to go to the process of making things such as pasta dough from scratch, it's a treat to have some leftover in the freezer.

MAKES ABOUT 1.3KG

175g fresh spinach

250g semolina flour

125ml plain flour

2 medium eggs

½ teaspoon sea salt

1. Steam the spinach and set aside to cool to room temperature. Squeeze the spinach in your fists to extract as much water as possible. Put the spinach in the bowl of a food processor fitted with a metal blade and chop to a paste.

2. Combine the semolina and plain flours on a flat work surface. Make a crater in the centre of the flour and crack the eggs into the crater. Add the spinach and salt and work them in with a fork until no flour is visible. Add 1 tablespoon water and knead the dough, gradually adding a further 2 tablespoons water, or more as needed (you want it to be moist like Play-Doh but not wet or sticky), for about 10 minutes until the dough feels elastic. Form the dough into a ball and wrap it tightly with clingfilm. Chill the dough in the fridge for about an hour. Roll out the dough with a rolling pin, then pass it through a pasta machine and cut or form the pasta dough to whatever shape your heart desires. Remember: the thinner the pasta the shorter the cook time.

Arrabiata Sauce

Arrabiata means 'angry' in Italian and refers to a simple, spicy tomato sauce flecked with red pepper flakes for heat. I lived in Rome for a while, so I've tried all the traditional Italian sauces. But, as I'm not Italian, I don't feel the need to stick to tradition. Back in Los Angeles, when I decided to make an arrabiata sauce, I thought: I live in California, so I might as well use what's available to me. For my arrabiata, I made this spicy, chunky tomato sauce using habanero peppers and chilli oil for heat instead of chilli flakes. I toss the sauce with pasta (you can use any dried pasta shape) on its own, and also use it along with shredded oxtail to make a spicy, meaty ragù.

MAKES ABOUT 1KG

1 tablespoon chilli oil

1 tablespoon olive oil

1.1kg Spanish onion (about 4 large onions), diced

2 tablespoons sea salt, plus more to taste

½ red pepper, cored, deseeded and diced

2 habanero chillies

2 garlic cloves, very finely chopped

1.3kg heirloom or vine-ripened red tomatoes, diced

120ml red wine

250g ready-made tomato pasta sauce

2 sprigs of fresh rosemary

15g fresh basil leaves

2 tablespoons dried oregano

2 tablespoons black pepper

1 teaspoon smoked paprika

1 recipe Fresh Spinach Pasta (see opposite)

1. Heat the chilli oil and olive oil in a large sauté pan over a medium heat. Sauté the onions in the pan, seasoning them with some of the salt and stirring often, for about 15 minutes until they are tender and caramelised (dark golden brown). Add the red pepper, habanero chillies and garlic, season them with some of the remaining salt and sauté, stirring often, for about 3 minutes until the pepper and chillies are soft. Pour in the wine and cook for 1 minute, stirring up any brown bits on the base of the pan. Add the tomatoes, season with the remaining salt and cook for about 5 minutes until they soften and break down. Stir in the tomato sauce, rosemary, basil, oregano, black pepper, 120ml water and paprika, reduce the heat to low and simmer for about 15 minutes to meld the flavours.

2. To cook the pasta, take half the recipe opposite, roll into a sheet using a pasta machine and then cut into linguine or spaghetti. Boil a large pan of well-salted water, drop in the pasta and cook for 6 minutes or until just al dente. Drain and serve in bowls with the sauce on the top.

Crab & Ricotta Ravioli
with Roasted Pepper Sauce

I worked in a restaurant in Los Angeles for a short period of time, and one of my jobs was to make the crab mousse ravioli. I didn't actually like the mousse, but I got really good at making ravioli – because I made hundreds of them. You can serve these as a main course, or, if you're doing an Italian themed night, serve just two or three on a plate as an appetiser. You can also flash fry them, which is a really special treat.

SERVES 4 AS A MAIN DISH; 8 AS A STARTER

15g unsalted butter

2 large shallots, very finely chopped

2 teaspoons sea salt, plus more for the pasta water

225g cooked white crabmeat

225g ricotta

¼ teaspoon dried chilli flakes

1 recipe Spinach Pasta Dough (page 125)

Semolina flour for dusting

2 medium egg yolks

1 recipe Roasted Pepper Sauce (page 128)

Wedge of Parmesan cheese for grating

Extra virgin olive oil for serving

1. Melt the butter with the shallots in a medium sauté pan over a medium heat. Sprinkle the shallots with 1 teaspoon of the salt and sauté for 10 minutes until soft and caramelised, stirring often so that they don't crisp. Set the shallots aside to cool to room temperature.

2. Combine the crab, ricotta, chilli flakes, caramelised shallots and the remaining teaspoon of salt in a large bowl and gently fold the ingredients together using a rubber spatula to ensure a light and fluffy filling.

3. Roll out the spinach pasta dough into 3mm-thick sheets. Stack the sheets on a baking tray, sprinkling with semolina flour between each sheet to keep them from sticking together.

4. Whisk the egg yolks with 2 tablespoons water to make an egg wash.

5. You can make ravioli in whatever size or shape you want using a ravioli or biscuit cutter. For 5cm-square ravioli, lay a sheet of pasta on your work surface. Brush a light layer of egg wash over the surface of the dough. Spoon 2 teaspoons of the filling in mounds along the centre of the dough, leaving 4cm between each mound. Put a second piece of dough on top. Use a ravioli cutter to cut between the mounds to make individual ravioli. Pinch the edges of the dough together to seal, transfer to a baking tray and dust with semolina flour until you're ready to boil the ravioli. Continue making ravioli until you've used all of the filling. Any leftover pasta dough will keep, wrapped in clingfilm in the fridge, for several days or you can freeze it.

6. To cook the ravioli, bring a large saucepan of water to the boil and salt it well. Drop the ravioli into the water and cook for 1–2 minutes until the pasta is tender. Lift the ravioli out of the water with a slotted spoon or strainer and transfer them to kitchen paper to drain.

7. To serve, spoon 60ml or 120ml of the sauce on each plate (amount varies depending on if you're serving the ravioli as a starter or a main dish). Lay the ravioli over the sauce, dribble with a little extra virgin olive oil and grate Parmesan on top.

Roasted Pepper Sauce

I made this sauce as something that would be my answer to traditional Italian tomato-vodka sauce. Instead of tomatoes, it's made with roasted red peppers, which I love. The resulting sauce is rich, delicious, flavourful, and colourful. And another thing: it's not acidic like tomato sauce is. I serve it with Crab Ravioli (page 127) but it also makes an amazing sauce to serve alongside chicken.

MAKES ABOUT 875G

3 red peppers

40g unsalted butter

1 red onion, chopped

1 teaspoon sea salt, plus more to taste

4 garlic cloves, very finely chopped

1 tablespoon black pepper

1 teaspoon Sofrito (page 75)

240ml low-salt chicken stock

240ml whipping cream

½ teaspoon dried oregano

50g Parmesan cheese, grated

1. Put the red peppers directly on the burner of a gas hob over a high heat for 8–10 minutes until they are charred on all sides and collapsed, turning with tongs to cook evenly. (Alternatively, roast the peppers under a preheated grill or in a 200°C/gas mark 6 oven until they have charred all over and collapsed.) Set the charred peppers aside in a bowl, covered tightly with clingfilm, to steam for 10–15 minutes. (Steaming makes them easier to peel.) Peel the peppers and remove and discard the cores.

2. Melt the butter in a large sauté pan over a medium-low heat. Add the red onion, season with ½ teaspoon of the salt and sauté, stirring often, for about 10 minutes until tender and translucent. Add the garlic, pepper, sofrito and roasted peppers, season with the remaining ½ teaspoon salt and sauté for 2 minutes until the garlic is fragrant, stirring constantly so that the garlic doesn't brown. Stir in the chicken stock, cream and oregano. Bring the liquid to the boil over a medium heat, reduce the heat and simmer for 10 minutes to thicken the liquid. Set aside to cool for at least 5 minutes. Transfer the contents of the sauté pan to the jug of a blender and purée until smooth. Sprinkle in the Parmesan and pulse to combine. Season with more salt to taste.

Fried Lobster Tails
with Garlic Aïoli Tartar Sauce

The first time I ever had deep-fried lobster tails was at a really nice restaurant in Georgia. I'm more of a crustacean person than a fish person myself, so when I saw fried lobster tails on the menu, it seemed like the obvious choice. It's so decadent and indulgent, it almost seems rude. When you serve it to friends, they're always excited by the idea. Fried. Lobster. Now that's luxury. You will need four wooden skewers for deep-frying the lobster tails.

SERVES 4

Rapeseed or vegetable oil for deep-frying—lots!

190g plain flour

2 teaspoons sea salt

½ teaspoon black pepper

70g cornmeal

1 teaspoon sea salt

4 raw lobster tails

2 medium eggs, lightly beaten

1 recipe Garlic Aïoli-Tartar Sauce (see below)

1. Fill a large saucepan with oil and heat the oil over a medium-high heat until it reaches 180°C. On the work surface, create a bed of kitchen paper.

2. Meanwhile, pour 125g of the flour into a medium bowl. Add the salt and pepper and stir to combine. Whisk the eggs in a second bowl. Mix the remaining 65g flour with the cornmeal in a third bowl.

3. Remove the top and bottom shells of the lobster tails, but leave the ends of the tails intact. Dredge each tail in the seasoned flour, dip it in the beaten egg, then dredge it in the flour-cornmeal mixture. Run a wooden skewer through each tail and cut the skewer so that it doesn't stick out more than 2.5cm on each side of the tail.

4. Carefully drop each lobster tail into the oil and fry for about 5 minutes until golden brown and crisp. Transfer the tails to the kitchen paper to drain. Remove and discard the skewers from the lobster tails and serve hot, with the aïoli on the side for dipping.

Garlic Aïoli-Tartar Sauce

Being a saucier, I've made aïoli a million ways. So many different combos can bring something simple to life.

MAKES ABOUT 500G

4 medium egg yolks

360ml olive oil

2 tablespoons fresh lemon juice

1 teaspoon very finely chopped garlic

½ teaspoon sea salt, plus more to taste

½ teaspoon black pepper

¼ teaspoon dried chilli flakes

70g dill pickled gherkins, finely chopped

½ celery stick, finely chopped

1. Put the egg yolks in a glass or stainless steel mixing bowl that fits over a medium saucepan. Fill the saucepan halfway with water and bring the water to the boil over a high heat. Remove the pan from the heat and place the bowl with the egg yolks on the pan. (If there is so much water in the pan that the base of the bowl touches the water, pour out some of the water.) Whisk the egg yolks to break them up.

2. Add one third of the the oil slowly, whisking to form an emulsion. Add a few drops of the lemon juice and continue whisking. Whisk in the remaining oil. Add the remaining lemon juice, garlic, salt, pepper and chilli flakes and whisk to combine. Stir in the gherkin and celery. Season with more salt to taste.

King Prawns
in Salsa Criolla with Strawberries

Salsa criolla is one of my favourite sauces. I used to serve it with chicken, but when travelling more, I noticed that a lot of cultures make salsa criolla with fish. When I lived in Spain we would eat whole fish in a rich, red salsa criolla; it was beautiful. There are so many different versions of it depending on where you are in the world. I started adding strawberries one summer when having a Labour Day barbecue for friends and was making the sauce in a massive pot; there, on the counter, were strawberries and I thought, 'What a beautiful, robust summer dish. The red strawberries with the yellow peppers, the green rosemary.' With all those colours, it's really a gorgeous dish. To me, this is what food should look like.

SERVES 4

2 tablespoons rapeseed oil

¾ teaspoon chilli oil

½ large Spanish onion, thinly sliced

1½ teaspoons sea salt, plus more to taste

½ bunch of small carrots, peeled and thinly sliced lengthways

4 garlic cloves, sliced

½ green, ½ red and ½ yellow pepper, cored, deseeded and thinly sliced

2 large vine-ripened tomatoes, chopped

¼ teaspoon black pepper, plus more to taste

½ teaspoon ground cumin

½ teaspoon hot smoked paprika

½ teaspoon sweet smoked paprika

2 sprigs of fresh rosemary

2 tablespoons Sofrito (page 75)

900g raw king prawns in their shells, deveined

½ teaspoon achiote paste, crumble

240ml vegetable stock or water (or cooking water from Mashed Plantains, page 68)

140g large strawberries, hulled and halved

1. In a large saucepan, heat 1 tablespoon of the rapeseed oil with half of the chilli oil over a medium-high heat. Add the onion, season with ½ teaspoon of the salt and cook, stirring, for about 5 minutes until it begins to soften. Add the carrots and cook for about 5 minutes until they begin to soften. Add the garlic and green, red and yellow peppers and cook for about 5 minutes until soft. Stir in the tomatoes, then sprinkle in the cumin, both paprikas and rosemary. Reduce the heat to low and simmer for about 10 minutes until all the vegetables are soft and fragrant. Season with more salt and the pepper and set aside.

2. Meanwhile, heat the remaining chilli oil in another large sauté pan. Add the sofrito and cook for about 1 minute until heated through. Add the prawns, sprinkle with the achiote and stir to mix thoroughly. Pour in the stock and simmer for about 5 minutes until the prawns turn pink and opaque, adding the strawberries halfway through. Then put the sautéed vegetables back into the pan with the prawns, stir to combine and serve.

Ginger Sesame Glazed Prawns with Pak Choi

I started making this prawn dish as a really quick and delicious meal, using my Bounty & Full Ginger Glaze. It obviously takes a bit longer if you make the sauce from scratch, but it's totally worth the time. It's an Asian dish that looks really beautiful, as though it has a load of little jewels in it.

SERVES 4

3 tablespoons toasted sesame oil

1 green pepper, cored, deseeded and thinly sliced

1¼ teaspoons sea salt, plus more to taste

4 large garlic cloves, thinly sliced

280g extra-large raw prawns, peeled and deveined

2 heads of pak choi, ends trimmed and quartered

120ml homemade Ginger Sesame Glaze (page 90)

30g pomegranate seeds (optional; you can substitute dried cherries or dried cranberries)

1. Heat 1 tablespoon of the sesame oil in a large sauté pan over a medium heat. Add the green pepper and garlic, season with ¼ teaspoon of the salt and cook for about 3 minutes until the pepper softens, stirring often so that the garlic doesn't brown.

2. Increase the heat to medium-high, add the remaining 2 tablespoons sesame oil and the prawns, season with the remaining 1 teaspoon salt and cook for about 5 minutes until the prawns are pink and cooked throughout.

3. Pour in the sesame glaze and toss to coat the prawns with the glaze.

4. Add the pak choi and cook for 2–3 minutes until it wilts. Season with more salt to taste.

5. Serve the prawns with the pomegranate seeds sprinkled on top, if you are using them.

Prawn Étouffée

I was reacquainted with prawn étouffée not long ago, when doing a show in New Orleans. I forgot how delicious it was and, after eating it there, came home and made it for my family. It's so good, and it's easy to make. If you start with fresh prawn in the shell, you can use the shells to make prawn stock. I'm a big believer in 'do what you can', so if you don't have time to make stock, use vegetable stock or store-bought fish stock instead. Just make sure you get the freshest prawns you can.

SERVES 4

For the stock

700g extra-large raw prawns

1 large onion, cut into chunks

1 celery stick, cut into chunks

1 carrot, cut into chunks

For the étouffée

115g unsalted butter

65g flour

2 large yellow onions, diced

4 teaspoons sea salt, plus more to taste

3 vine-ripened or heirloom tomatoes

1 red pepper, cored, deseeded and diced

1 yellow pepper, cored, deseeded and diced

2 celery sticks, diced

1½ tablespoons chopped garlic
(from about 6 cloves)

3 dried bay leaves

2 teaspoons chopped fresh oregano

1 teaspoon fresh thyme leaves

½ teaspoon cayenne pepper

1. To make the stock, peel and devein the prawns, reserving the prawn shells and tails. Cover the prawns and refrigerate.

2. Put the prawn shells and tails in a large saucepan. Add the onion, celery, red or yellow pepper and carrot and enough water to cover by several centimetres. Bring the water to the boil over a high heat, reduce the heat and simmer, skimming off the impurities that rise to the top, for 1 hour. Strain and discard the contents of the colander.

3. To make the étouffée, melt the butter with the flour in a large flameproof casserole dish or another large heavy-based pan over a medium heat and cook, stirring constantly so that the flour doesn't burn, for about 10 minutes until the flour is the colour of caramel.

4. Add the onions with 1 teaspoon of the salt and cook for about 5 minutes, stirring often, to soften. Add the tomatoes, red and yellow peppers, celery, garlic, bay leaves, oregano, thyme, cayenne and 1 teaspoon of the remaining salt and cook for 2–3 minutes to break down the tomatoes.

5. Stir in the stock and the remaining 2 teaspoons salt and bring to the boil over a high heat. Reduce the heat and simmer for about 45 minutes until the liquid begins to thicken.

6. Add the prawns and cook for 5–7 minutes until they are cooked through. Season with more salt to taste. Serve hot.

Knight-Style Tuna Melt

This recipe is great and also works well with chicken or turkey. My son Knight loves to cook with me in the kitchen – he's my favourite helper. He loves tuna melts so we make this together. I love it too. It's a nice spin on a modern classic.

MAKES ENOUGH FOR 8 SANDWICHES

For the tuna salad

3 × 120g cans tuna in spring water, drained

40g golden raisins

¼ red onion, cut into small dice

1 celery stick, cut into small dice

¼ tart green apple, cut into small dice

1 tablespoon very finely chopped garlic

35g raw, unsalted pistachios, roughly chopped

90g mayonnaise

1½ tablespoons curry powder

1½ teaspoons sea salt, plus more to taste

¼ teaspoon cayenne pepper

For the sandwiches

4 sandwich-sized ciabatta rolls, split in half, or 8 slices rustic white or wholemeal bread

60g unsalted butter, softened at room temperature

4 slices of Emmenthal or Havarti cheese

1. To make the tuna salad, combine all of the tuna salad ingredients in a large bowl and mix to thoroughly combine.

2. If you're using ciabatta, butter the outer sides of the bread. If you're using sliced bread, butter one side of each slice. Put the ciabatta bottoms or 8 slices of the bread, buttered side down, on your work surface and spoon a quarter of the tuna salad on each. Lay a slice of cheese on each sandwich.

3. Heat a large frying pan over a medium heat. Working in batches that will fit in the frying pan, grill the sandwiches until they are golden and the cheese is melted. Serve hot.

Mango Chutney

I learnt a lot about chutney when I was in Kuala Lumpur some years ago. Until then, I didn't know that chutney is a broad term that refers to many types of condiments, and that what we think of as chutney is actually known in the East as 'English chutney'. Mango is a classic. I love it.

MAKES ABOUT 500G

1 teaspoon ghee (or unsalted butter)

½ yellow onion, chopped

½ teaspoon sea salt

1 large mango, peeled, stoned and diced

150g demerara sugar

1 tablespoon curry powder

2 teaspoons grated fresh ginger

½ teaspoon ground coriander

½ teaspoon ground cumin

1½ tablespoons apple cider vinegar

1. Heat the ghee in a medium saucepan over a medium heat for about 1 minute.

2. Add the onion, season with the salt and sauté, stirring constantly, for about 5 minutes until it begins to soften. Add the mango and cook for about 2 minutes.

3. Stir in the sugar, curry powder, ginger, coriander and cumin and cook, stirring, until the sugar melts and begins to bubble. Reduce the heat to medium-low and cook for 3–5 minutes, stirring often, until the sauce thickens. Stir through the vinegar and season with more salt to taste. It will keep, refrigerated, in an airtight container for a few months.

Mandarin Orange Cranberry Sauce

I'm proud to say that I've never eaten shop-bought cranberry sauce, ever. It never made sense to me, because cranberry sauce is so easy to make yourself, there's no reason not to. I cook the cranberries with vanilla to give it a nice round flavour, and add mandarin orange segments because I love the taste and the colours look so beautiful together. The other thing about cranberry sauce is: why do we only see it at Thanksgiving or Christmas? It's so tasty and versatile. I use it as a glaze for grilled prawns or roast chicken, spoon it into vinaigrettes if I want a touch of sweetness and add it to baked goods, such as Olive Oil Cranberry Cakes with Candied Orange Slices (page 151). This sauce is great in turkey, ham or roast beef sandwiches. I often serve it on a cheese board; it goes with just about any cheese. I pretty much always have some of this sauce in my fridge.

MAKES ABOUT 500G

300g granulated sugar

Grated zest of 4 mandarin oranges or 1 large orange, plus 240ml fresh squeezed mandarin or orange juice

¼ teaspoon sea salt

700g fresh or frozen cranberries

1 tablespoon pure vanilla extract

1. Combine the sugar, mandarin juice, 120ml water and salt in a medium saucepan and bring the liquid to the boil over a high heat. Stir in the cranberries, mandarin zest and vanilla. Reduce the heat to low and simmer for 20–30 minutes, stirring occasionally, until the cranberries have broken down and the juices have thickened to a sauce consistency. Serve the sauce warm or at room temperature. It will keep, refrigerated in an airtight container, for several weeks.

Whiskey Pear Glaze

This is a delicious sweet and savoury glaze for a smoked, clove-studded ham. Equally you can rub it on lamb or roast beef for a dinner part. I also use it with pork chops and apple sauce to kick things up a notch.

MAKES ABOUT 500G

3 pears, peeled, cored and chopped

1 tablespoon yellow onion, roughly chopped

1 garlic clove, smashed and roughly chopped

1 teaspoon sea salt

75g granulated sugar

300ml whisky

1 small sprig of fresh rosemary

3 whole cloves

1 cinnamon stick

½ teaspoon black pepper

1. Fill a large saucepan with 2.5cm water and bring to the boil over a high heat.

2. Cook the pears, onion, garlic and salt in the boiling water for a couple minutes. Sprinkle the sugar into the pan, stir to combine and cook, stirring occasionally, until the sauce begins to thicken. Stir in the whisky.

3. Add the rosemary, cloves, cinnamon stick and pepper and cook for about 5 minutes until the pears are soft and mushy. Discard the rosemary and cinnamon stick and set aside for 5 minutes to cool.

4. Purée in the jug of a blender or the bowl of a food processor fitted with a metal blade until smooth.

Pistachio Basil Pesto

Although they're great, sometimes pine nuts can be overpowering, so I love to use pistachios in pesto. It's not traditional, but pistachios are crunchy and they add to the green. This pesto looks beautiful and tastes amazing with a nutty flavour. I've visited Turkey and Israel, where they use pistachios a lot in desserts. I thought: what else can I do with them? That's when I started using pistachios instead of pine nuts. It turns out the pairing of pistachios and basil is fantastic.

MAKES ABOUT 500G

175g fresh basil

125g raw unsalted pistachios

530ml extra-virgin olive oil

6–8 garlic cloves, smashed and roughly chopped

50g fresh spinach

50g Parmesan cheese, finely grated

1 teaspoon sea salt, plus more to taste

1. Combine all of the ingredients in the bowl of a food processor fitted with a metal blade or the jug of a blender and purée. Season with more salt to taste.

Sweet treats

'I never knew the love that these could bring me.'

Cappuccino Cheesecake
with Gingernut Base & Dulce de Leche Topping

I make a lot of cheesecakes, but this is by far the most popular. I smear dulce de leche over the top and decorate the edges with chocolate chips. It's so rich and delicious. I prefer to use vanilla pods to vanilla extract. After scraping out the seeds, I put the pod in a bowl of sugar to make vanilla sugar. Or – a trick from the older ladies in the Dominican Republic – I put the scraped pods in a pot of water and simmer for the best air freshener ever. Latinos make dulce de leche by simmering a can of sweetened condensed milk for 3 hours. Nothing works better, and it couldn't be easier.

SERVES 8-10

For the base

75g unsalted butter, melted, plus more cold butter for greasing the tin

250g chocolate or gingernut biscuit crumbs

100–175g granulated sugar (depending on desired sweetness)

For the filling

500g cream cheese, softened at room temperature

450g mascarpone cheese, softened at room temperature

250g caster sugar

3 medium eggs

60ml brewed espresso, cooled to room temperature

2 heaped tablespoons plain flour

1 vanilla pod

For the topping

1 x 400g can sweetened condensed milk, label removed

90g dark chocolate (45–60 per cent cocoa) chips

Sea salt flakes for sprinkling

1. To make the base, position a shelf in the centre of the oven and preheat to 180°C/gas mark 4. Grease the inside of a 20 or 23cm springform tin. Wrap the outside of the pan with foil (this keeps water from leaking into the cheesecake when you bake it in a bain-marie).

2. Stir the biscuit crumbs, melted butter and sugar together in a medium bowl to combine. Press the crumb mixture to cover the base and up the sides of the prepared tin. Bake for 10 minutes and set aside to cool.

3. To make the filling, combine the cream cheese, mascarpone and sugar in the bowl of a stand mixer fitted with the whisk attachment. Cream on a medium-high speed until the mixture is light and fluffy and no lumps remain, stopping to scrape down the sides of the bowl with a rubber spatula every 2–3 minutes. Add the eggs one at a time, mixing on a medium speed after each addition until they are incorporated. Add the espresso and flour and mix on a medium speed to combine. Split the vanilla pod down the middle with a paring knife and scrape the seeds into the bowl. Mix on a medium speed until all of the ingredients are blended.

4. Put the springform tin in a baking dish and pour water 2.5cm up the sides of the tin. Pour the filling mixture into the pre-baked base, smooth the top and bake for 80–90 minutes until a skewer inserted into the centre comes out clean. (It will jiggle when you shake the tin; it sets as it cools.) Set aside in the bain-marie to cool to room temperature. Remove from the bain-marie, discard the foil and refrigerate for at least 3 hours.

5. Meanwhile, put the unopened can of condensed milk in a saucepan of water. Boil the can for 3 hours, making sure the can is submerged at all times. Remove the can and set it aside to allow the dulce de leche to cool for about 10 minutes in the can. It should be room temperature when added to the cheesecake.

6. When ready to serve, run a knife around the edges of the springform tin to loosen the cheesecake crust from the sides. Unlatch the tin and carefully remove the sides. Spread half of the dulce de leche over the top, sprinkle the chocolate chips around the edges and sprinkle with sea salt. Slice and serve chilled.

New York Vanilla Bean Cheesecake

I am known among my family, friends, and co-workers for my cheesecake. Being from New York, my mother makes a great cheesecake, so when I started making my own, I used her recipe as a jumping-off point. I add a bit of lemon zest, so the cheesecake is creamy and refreshing instead of just cheesy. Cheesecake is a great dessert to bring to a dinner party, because it makes a grand entrance, and everyone loves it. If I am bringing it somewhere, I top the cheesecake with fresh fruit, which makes the cheesecake look so pretty: it's like bringing dessert and flowers at the same time. The crust is made from Digestive biscuit crumbs, but if you want to mix things up, you can use any hard biscuit, such as gingersnaps or shortbread. If you use shortbread, add 2 tablespoons of ground pecans to the mix to give it a good texture and keep it from being too buttery.

COOK'S TIP: You will need an 8- or 9-inch springform pan to make this dessert.

SERVES 8–10

For the base

75g unsalted butter, melted and cooled to room temperature, plus more cold butter for greasing the tin

250g digestive biscuit crumbs crackers

100g granulated sugar

For the filling

500g cream cheese, softened at room temperature

450g mascarpone or ricotta cheese or soured cream, softened at room temperature

300g caster sugar

3 medium eggs

2 heaped tablespoons plain flour

1 vanilla pod

Finely grated zest of ½ lemon

1. To make the base, position an oven shelf in the centre and preheat the oven to 180°F/gas mark 4. Grease the inside (base and sides) of a 20cm or 23cm springform tin. Wrap the outside of the pan (base and sides) with foil (this keeps water from leaking into the cheesecake when you bake it in a bain-marie).

2. Stir the digestive biscuit crumbs, melted butter and sugar together in a medium bowl to combine. Using your hands, press the crumb mixture to cover the base and up the sides of the prepared tin. Bake the base for 10 minutes and set aside to cool to room temperature.

3. To make the filling, combine the cream cheese, mascarpone and sugar in the bowl of a stand mixer fitted with the whisk attachment. Cream on a medium-high speed for about 8 minutes until the mixture is light and fluffy and no lumps remain, stopping to scrape down the sides of the bowl with a rubber spatula every 2 or 3 minutes. Add the eggs one at a time,

mixing on a medium speed after each addition until all of the eggs are incorporated. Turn off the mixer. Add the flour and mix on a medium speed just to combine. Split the vanilla pod down the middle with a paring knife. Use the knife to scrape the seeds from the pod and into the bowl. Add the lemon zest and mix on a medium speed until all of the ingredients are blended.

4. For the baine-marie, put the springform tin in a baking dish and pour enough water to come 2.5cm up the sides of the tin. Pour the filling mixture into the pre-baked base, smooth the top with a rubber spatula and bake the cheesecake on the middle shelf for 80–90 minutes until a skewer inserted into the centre comes out clean. (Note that the cheesecake will still jiggle when you shake the tin; it will set as it cools.) Set the cheesecake aside in the bain-marie to cool to room temperature. Remove the cheesecake from the bain-marie, remove and discard the foil and refrigerate for at least 3 hours, or ideally, overnight to chill.

5. To remove the cheesecake from the springform tin, run a knife around the edges of the tin to loosen the crust from the sides. Unlatch the tin to release the cake and carefully remove the sides of the tin. Cut the cheesecake into 8 or 10 slices and serve chilled.

Skillet Cornbread with Crystallised Ginger

Last year, I asked my son what he wanted for his birthday and he said he didn't want anything except my cornbread. I baked it in little baby cast iron frying pans. They were so cute and he loved them.

I wake up in the middle of the night sometimes thinking '!!!' and just write down whatever the idea is in my phone. I've seen so many cornbread recipes, especially here in California where there's a lot of Mexican and South American influence. I wanted to add something that wasn't obvious. I couldn't think of anything, went to sleep, and it was like a light went on one night I woke thinking 'Crystallised ginger!'. That's how I make it now. It's such an unexpected but perfectly fitting flavour.

SERVES 8–10

For the cornbread

60g unsalted butter, melted

125g plain flour

140g cornmeal

1 teaspoon ground ginger

200g caster sugar

1 teaspoon baking powder

1 teaspoon bicarbonate of soda

1 teaspoon sea salt

240ml full-fat milk

1 large egg

2 heaped tablespoons mayonnaise

45g crystallised ginger, chopped

65g fresh sweetcorn kernels (from about 2 corn cobs) or canned or frozen, defrosted and drained

For the glaze

60g unsalted butter, melted

2 tablespoons runny honey

1 pinch sea salt

1. Preheat the oven to 180°C/gas mark 4. Pour the melted butter into a 25cm cast-iron (ovenproof) frying pan. Use a pastry brush or kitchen paper to grease the sides of the pan with the butter.

2. Reserve 1 tablespoon of the flour. In a large bowl, mix together the remaining flour, the cornmeal, ground ginger, sugar, baking powder, bicarbonate of soda and salt. In a small bowl, whisk the milk, eggs and mayonnaise together, then pour the wet ingredients into the bowl with the dry ingredients. In a small bowl, toss the crystallised ginger with the reserved tablespoon of flour and toss to coat. (This prevents the ginger from sinking to the base of the tin when the cornbread bakes.) Add the flour-coated ginger and any flour left in the bowl to the batter. Stir in the sweetcorn to evenly distribute.

3. Pour the batter into the prepared frying pan and bake for 35–40 minutes, or until a skewer inserted into the centre comes out clean.

4. Meanwhile, in a small bowl, whisk together the melted butter, honey and salt to make the glaze.

5. When the cornbread is done, remove it from the oven and use a fork to poke holes all over the surface. Brush the glaze over the cornbread with a pastry brush. (The glaze is best absorbed if you brush it on when the cornbread is hot out of the oven.) Leave the cornbread to cool slightly. Cut it into wedges and serve.

Sweetcorn Fritters

These started out as traditional savoury corn fritters. I made them as a fun treat for my son and his cousin, who was staying the night. To make banana-strawberry fritters, which they absolutely love, substitute 225g mashed banana and 40g chopped strawberries for the corn in this recipe.

We have fresh corn three quarters of the year – if you can't find it fresh, use frozen, as the tinned corn is pasteurised and loses a lot of its properties.

MAKES ABOUT 16 FRITTERS; SERVES 6-8

2 medium eggs

120ml full-fat milk

125g plain flour

50g granulated sugar

1 teaspoon baking powder

1 teaspoon bicarbonate of soda

1 teaspoon ground cinnamon

½ teaspoon ground nutmeg

½ teaspoon sea salt

135g fresh sweetcorn kernels (from about 4 corn cobs) or canned or frozen corn, defrosted and drained

Rapeseed or vegetable oil for deep-frying

Icing sugar for dusting

1. Whisk the eggs in a large bowl to break up the yolks, then whisk in the milk. In a separate, medium bowl, stir together the flour, granulated sugar, baking powder, bicarbonate of soda, cinnamon, nutmeg and salt to thoroughly combine. Add the flour mixture to the bowl with the eggs and milk and stir until no flour is visible. Stir the sweetcorn into the batter to evenly distribute.

2. Heat 7.5-10cm of oil in a medium saucepan until it reaches 180°C. Make a bed of kitchen paper.

3. Using a tablespoon, scoop a heaped tablespoon of the batter and use a second tablespoon to push the batter into the oil. Drop as many fritters as will fit in a single layer in the oil without crowding the pan and fry them until golden brown. (Depending on the size of the pan you're using, you will need to fry two or three batches of fritters.) Using a slotted spoon, transfer the fritters to the kitchen paper to drain. Dust with icing sugar and fry the remaining batter in the same way.

Ricotta American Biscuits

Before I went to culinary school, baking was not something I did, ever. It was so daunting to me, the way ingredients interacted with one another in the oven. In school, I began to understand the fundamentals of baking, and now I feel much more comfortable with it. I even feel comfortable enough to play around with classic recipes, which is what I did with these biscuits. I use ricotta and yogurt in place of buttermilk, which is the standard. Ricotta is such a light, wonderful, fluffy cheese – it works magic in the biscuits. For heartier biscuits, add 35g of 5mm-cubed cured chorizo, or any sort of meat, to the dough.

MAKES 7 OR 8 BISCUITS

1. Whisk the ricotta, yogurt, milk and egg together in a large bowl until thoroughly blended.

2. In the bowl of a food processor with a metal blade attachment, pulse the flour, baking powder and salt to combine. Add the butter and pulse until the mixture resembles fine breadcrumbs. Transfer the contents of the food processor to a large bowl. Add the ricotta mixture and mix with a fork until no flour is visible. Bring the dough together into a ball with floured hands, wrap in clingfilm and refrigerate for 30 minutes.

125g ricotta

60ml natural full-fat yogurt

60ml full-fat milk

1 medium egg

275g plain flour, plus more for dusting

2 teaspoons baking powder

1¼ teaspoons sea salt

170g cold unsalted butter, cut into small cubes

1 medium egg yolk beaten with
  1 tablespoon water to make an egg wash

3. Position an oven shelf in the centre and preheat the oven to 180°C/gas mark 4.

4. Dust a flat work surface or wooden cutting board with flour. Unwrap the chilled dough and place it on the floured work surface. With a floured rolling pin, roll out the dough into a 1cm-thick rectangle. Fold the sides towards the centre in thirds. Return the dough to the fridge for 10 minutes and then roll it out again into a 1cm-thick rectangle. Use a 5–7.5cm round biscuit cutter (or a small glass) to cut out 7 or 8 biscuits. Put them on an ungreased baking tray, leaving 2.5cm spaces between them. Brush the tops of the biscuits with the egg wash and bake for 12–14 minutes until the tops are golden brown. Serve warm.

Coconut Custard Pie

This is a dessert that my mum used to make for my sisters and me when we were growing up. I've tweaked it over the years by adding chocolate chips and vanilla. I also add more coconut flakes to the custard than my mum does, because I love coconut more than I love custard. This is the dessert I make most often when I decide to have people for dinner at the last minute and need to throw something together. It's easy to make and the ingredients are always on hand, including shop-bought frozen pastry for just such times.

SERVES 8

3 medium eggs

240ml whipping cream

480ml sweet coconut cream (shake can before opening)

100g caster sugar

1 tablespoon pure vanilla extract

45g sweetened coconut flakes

90g dark chocolate chips

Buttery Flaky Everything Dough (page 157), rolled and fitted into a 23cm pie plate (or 1 ready-made shop-bought pastry case)

1. Position an oven shelf in the centre and preheat the oven to 190°C/gas mark 5.

2. Whisk the eggs in a bowl to break up the yolks. Add the cream, coconut cream, sugar, melted butter and vanilla and whisk to combine. Stir in the coconut flakes.

3. Put the pastry case on a baking tray. Scatter the chocolate chips over the base of the pastry case and pour the filling on top, smoothing with a rubber spatula. Bake on the centre shelf for 10 minutes. Reduce the heat to 160°C/gas mark 3 and bake for a further 45–50 minutes, until the custard is set. Cool to room temperature before slicing and serving.

Olive Oil Cranberry Cakes with Crystallised Oranges

This is definitely one of my favourites. I make a lot of breads and desserts, and people ask me to bake quite often. Olive oil keeps the cake moist and gives it a rich texture.

COOK'S TIP: You will need sixteen 2-inch ramekins to make these little cakes.

MAKES 16 INDIVIDUAL CAKES

For the crystallised oranges

500g granulated sugar

2 oranges, halved and cut into 3mm-thick slices

For the cakes

155g plain flour

1 teaspoon baking powder

½ teaspoon bicarbonate of soda

½ teaspoon sea salt

2 medium eggs

150g caster sugar

80ml extra virgin olive oil, plus more for greasing the ramekins

Grated zest of 1 orange plus 80ml fresh orange juice (from 1 orange)

1 teaspoon pure vanilla extract

165g Mandarin Orange Cranberry Sauce (page 138; or shop-bought cranberry sauce)

For the glaze

85g unsalted butter, melted

½ teaspoon pure vanilla extract

75g sifted icing sugar

1. Position an oven shelf in the centre and preheat the oven to 180°C/gas mark 4. Grease the ramekins with olive oil and set them aside on a baking tray.

2. To make the crystallised oranges, line a baking tray with baking parchment. Sprinkle the parchment with 50g of the granulated sugar and set aside.

3. Put the remaining 450g granulated sugar in a mound in the centre of a small saucepan. Pour 6 tablespoons water over the mound, letting it seep in until it looks like wet sand. Cook over a medium heat without stirring for about 8 minutes until the sugar has melted and starts to bubble. Add the orange slices and simmer until they look glossy and the pulp is translucent. Turn off the heat and use tongs to remove the syrup-coated slices from the saucepan, arranging them in a single layer on the sugar-coated baking tray. Set aside.

4. To make the cakes, combine the flour, baking powder, bicarbonate of soda and salt in a large bowl and set aside. In the bowl of a stand mixer fitted with a paddle attachment, mix the eggs just to break up the yolks. Add the caster sugar, olive oil, orange juice and vanilla and mix to incorporate. Turn off the mixer, add half of the dry ingredients and mix on a low speed until no flour is visible. Add the remaining dry ingredients and mix on a low speed until no flour is visible, then add the cranberry sauce and orange zest to thoroughly combine.

5. Pour the batter into the prepared ramekins and put the baking tray on the centre shelf to bake for 12–15 minutes until a skewer inserted into one of the cakes comes out clean. Set the baking tray on a wire rack and leave the cakes to cool to room temperature.

6. Meanwhile, make the glaze. Stir the melted butter and vanilla together in a medium bowl. Add the icing sugar and whisk until no lumps remain.

7. When the cakes have cooled, carefully pop them out of the ramekins onto a baking tray so that the bases are facing up. Using the back of a spoon, spread the glaze over the cakes, dividing it evenly. Decorate with the crystallised orange slices.

Oatmeal Wholemeal Pancakes with Cherries

Black cherries are super-sweet and I use them to make a gorgeous barbecue sauce. Their season is so short. The darker the colour, the better the cherries are for you as they contain more antioxidants. These are my favourite pancakes, and not just because they're (sort of) healthy.

MAKES ABOUT 12 PANCAKES

60g quick-cooking porridge oats

150ml whipping cream

100g wholemeal flour

1½ teaspoons sea salt

1½ teaspoons baking powder

3/4 teaspoon bicarbonate of soda

1 teaspoon ground cinnamon

120ml full-fat milk

25g unsalted butter, melted and cooled to room temperature, plus more cold butter for cooking the pancakes

1 medium egg

1 packed tablespoon soft light or dark brown sugar

1 teaspoon pure vanilla extract

360g stoned and roughly chopped fresh or frozen dark or red cherries (or substitute blackberries or blueberries)

Maple syrup for serving

1. Combine the oats and 120ml of the cream in a medium bowl and set aside for 10 minutes to soften the oats.

2. Meanwhile, stir together the flour, salt, baking powder, bicarbonate of soda and cinnamon in a large bowl to thoroughly combine. Add the milk, melted butter, egg, sugar, vanilla and the remaining 30ml (2 tablespoons) cream. Mix with a spatula until the wet and dry ingredients are combined. Add the softened oats to the bowl and gently fold in the cherries.

3. Heat a griddle or frying pan over a medium heat. Add some butter and let it melt. Pour 60ml of the batter into the pan for each pancake and cook for 2–3 minutes per side, until deep golden on both sides, flipping only once. Serve warm with maple syrup.

Chocolate Chip Cookies
with Sea Salt Potato Crisps

I love salty and sweet together, so it's not surprising that, when someone gave me a dark chocolate-dipped crisp, I thought it was the best thing I'd ever tasted. Not long after, I was making chocolate chip cookies to take to a friend's baby shower and I came up with the idea of adding crumbled crisps to the cookie dough. The cookies turned out amazingly, and now crisps are a standard addition to my chocolate chip cookies. I like to use very dark, semi-sweet chocolate, going to the market and buying big chunks of it and chopping it up to store in a tin; otherwise I buy packaged chocolate chunks, not chips, for these because big pieces melt into the cookies better.

INGREDIENT NOTE: It's important to use artisanal crisps; something a bit thicker than old-school super-thin ones. Crumble them until the pieces are the size of cornflakes.

MAKES ABOUT 48 COOKIES

450g unsalted butter, softened at room temperature

440g soft light or dark brown sugar

400g granulated sugar

2 medium eggs

2 teaspoons pure vanilla extract

2 teaspoons hot water

375g plain flour

1½ tablespoons cocoa powder

1 teaspoon bicarbonate of soda

1 teaspoon fine sea salt

350g good-quality dark chocolate, 70% cocoa solids, chopped into 1cm chunks

100g crumbled gourmet potato crisps (see Ingredient Note)

Sea salt flakes for sprinkling

1. Position one oven shelf in the lower third and another in the upper third of the oven. Preheat to 160°C/gas mark 3.

2. In the bowl of a stand mixer fitted with the paddle attachment, mix the butter and both sugars on a medium-high speed for about 10 minutes until light and fluffy, stopping every few minutes to scrape down the sides of the bowl with a rubber spatula. Add the eggs, vanilla and hot water and mix to combine.

3. In a large bowl, stir together the flour, cocoa powder, bicarbonate of soda and salt. Add the dry ingredients to the bowl of the mixer and mix on a low speed until no flour is visible. Stir in the chocolate chunks and 70g of the potato crisp crumbles.

4. Scoop heaped tablespoons of the dough (about 4cm each) onto an ungreased baking tray, leaving at least 5cm between them. Sprinkle a pinch of sea salt flakes and press a few of the remaining potato crisp crumbles on each dough ball.

5. Bake for 12-14 minutes until the cookies are golden brown, rotating the baking trays from front to back and from the upper and lower shelves halfway through for even baking. Set the cookies aside to cool slightly before removing them from the baking tray. Bake the remaining dough in the same way.

Apple Pie

I have very strong opinions about apple pie. I like it very sweet, I add lots of butter – that's what makes it delicious and brings perfect colour to the crust – and the apples should be very soft and gooey. That's how I grew up eating it. Cook the green apples down. They hold their texture and they're still identifiable. You just let them get bubbly and caramelly – terrific!

SERVES 8

1.3–1.6kg Granny Smith apples or other tart apples, peeled, cored and sliced 2cm thick

150g granulated sugar

165g soft light or dark brown sugar

1½ teaspoons ground cinnamon

½ teaspoon freshly grated nutmeg

3 heaped tablespoons plain flour, plus more for dusting

1 recipe Buttery Flaky Everything Dough (page 157), chilled

115g cold unsalted butter, cubed

Vanilla ice cream for serving

1. Position an oven shelf in the centre and preheat the oven to 200°C/gas mark 6.

2. In a large bowl, toss the apples with both sugars, the cinnamon and nutmeg to coat. Sprinkle the flour over the apples and toss to distribute. Set aside while you make the pastry case.

3. Dust a flat work surface with flour. Remove one disc of the dough (half of the recipe) from the fridge and place it on the flour-dusted surface. Dust a rolling pin with flour and roll out the dough into a 30cm circle. Fold the dough in half, lift it into a 24cm pie dish and unfold it to cover the dish. Using scissors, trim the dough, leaving 2.5cm of dough hanging over the edge of the dish. Remove the second disc from the fridge and roll it out in the same way. Pour the apple mixture into the prepared pastry case, smoothing with a rubber spatula to evenly distribute it. Scatter the cubes of butter over the apples. Carefully lift the remaining dough disc and centre it on top of the pie. Trim the dough using scissors so that 2.5cm of dough hangs over the edge; fold the excess dough under itself to form a thick rim around the edge of the pie. Using your thumb and forefinger, pinch thick mountain peaks around the edges of the pastry to seal it. Use a small sharp knife to cut a hole or an X in the centre of the pastry lid to allow steam to escape while the pie is baking. Put the pie on a baking tray and bake it on the centre shelf for about 1 hour until the pastry is golden brown. Set the pie aside to cool slightly before serving. Cut into wedges and serve with ice cream.

Buttery Flaky Everything Dough

This is a standard flaky, buttery pie dough. I add a teaspoon of sugar, which is just enough to bring out the flavour of the butter without making the crust sweet.

MAKES ENOUGH FOR 2 PASTRY CASES, OR 1 DOUBLE-CRUST PIE

300g plain flour

1 teaspoon granulated sugar

1 teaspoon sea salt

225g cold, unsalted butter, cut into cubes

about 4 tablespoons iced water, or more as needed

1. Combine the flour, sugar and salt in a large bowl and mix to distribute the sugar and salt.

2. Add the butter and rub it into the flour with your fingertips until the mixture resembles breadcrumbs. Add 2 tablespoons of the iced water and continue mixing, adding more water as necessary to bring the dough together into a ball.

3. Divide the ball in half and pat each half to form a disc. Wrap each disc in clingfilm and refrigerate for at least 1 hour or up to several days. You can wrap any extra dough in clingfilm and freeze.

Goat's Cheese Ice Cream

In culinary school, we had this amazing restaurant-quality ice-cream maker, and I got so excited about it that I started using it to make every flavour of ice cream you could imagine. I love good cheese, especially goat's cheese, so during that ice cream-obsessed period of my life, making this was just a natural thing. It's actually light when you taste it, very creamy, and it doesn't get very hard – its consistency is more like gelato.

COOK'S TIP: This recipe requires an ice cream maker.

SERVES 6–8

4 medium egg yolks

200g caster sugar

480ml whipping cream

120ml full-fat milk

115g goat's cheese, crumbled

3 tablespoons light corn syrup

1. Whisk the egg yolks and sugar in a medium bowl for 4–5 minutes until they are pale yellow. Set aside.

2. Heat the cream and milk in a medium saucepan over a medium heat, stirring constantly, for about 5 minutes until small bubbles form at the edge. Turn off the heat. Gradually add one-quarter of the hot cream mixture to the bowl with the egg yolk mixture to temper the eggs, stirring constantly with a whisk to prevent the hot cream from cooking the eggs. Make a custard by gradually adding the tempered eggs to the saucepan of milk and cream, whisking constantly. Cook the custard over a medium-low heat, stirring constantly with a whisk, for about 10 minutes until it is thick enough to coat the back of a spoon. Pass the custard through a fine-mesh sieve into a bowl. Place the bowl over an ice bath for about 30 minutes until the custard cools completely.

3. Meanwhile, combine the goat's cheese with the corn syrup in a small mixing bowl. Add a cupful of the custard and whisk the ingredients until no lumps of goat's cheese remain. Stir the goat's cheese mixture into the bowl of custard. Cover and refrigerate for at least 2 hours or ideally overnight until completely cooled.

4. Pour the ice-cream mixture into an ice-cream maker and churn according to the manufacturer's instructions. For the best results, serve straight from the ice-cream maker.

Peach Blackberry Buckle

I'm more of a savoury than pastry chef, but when I have people over for dinner I make everything I serve. This dessert becomes a fruity, doughy, delicious mess, warm and comforting. You just pour the batter into the pan, put the fruit on top, and the oven does the rest. The tops and edges turn crispy and golden brown, and the centre is soft and heavy with fruit. We have white peaches in LA but I prefer the yellow ones because they're sweeter and have a stronger flavour. Frozen peaches work as well. Served warm, with vanilla ice cream, this buckle is so impressive that people will think you've been baking all day.

COOK'S TIP: use 8 miniature cast-iron frying pans or 12cm ramekins, or make a full-sized buckle using a deep pie dish or casserole dish as I have here.

SERVES 8

For the fruit

115g unsalted butter

200g demerara sugar

1 teaspoon sea salt

2 tablespoons pure vanilla extract

1 teaspoon ground cinnamon

1 teaspoon ground nutmeg

150–175g stoned and skinned peaches

300g frozen blackberries

For the batter

130g wholemeal flour

200g demerara sugar

1 teaspoon baking powder

½ teaspoon sea salt

240ml full-fat milk

115g unsalted butter

Vanilla ice cream for serving

1. Position an oven shelf in the centre of the oven and preheat the oven to 180°C/gas mark 4.

2. To prepare the fruit, combine the butter, sugar, salt, vanilla, cinnamon and nutmeg in a large saucepan over a medium heat and cook until the sugar dissolves. Add the peaches, stir to coat them with the sugar mixture, and cook for 1 minute. Turn off the heat and set aside.

3. To make the batter, in a large bowl, combine the flour, sugar, baking powder and salt and stir to distribute them evenly. Pour in the milk and mix until the dry ingredients are moistened.

4. Cut the butter into 1-tablespoon pieces and put a piece in each mini frying pan or ramekin (or put the whole amount of butter in the base of a large, deep pie dish or casserole dish). Put the pans or ramekins on a baking tray and heat in the oven for about 10 minutes until the butter begins to bubble. If you are using mini frying pans, carefully pour the batter to come to just below the rim of each. If you are using ramekins, fill them half full. If you're making one big buckle, pour all of the batter into the large dish.

5. Gently stir the blackberries into the pan with the peaches and spoon the fruit mixture over the batter, dividing it evenly if you are making small buckles. Return the baking tray to the oven and bake until golden brown, about 20 minutes for individual buckles; 35–40 minutes for a large buckle. Remove the baking tray from the oven and set aside to cool slightly before serving. Serve warm with vanilla ice cream.

Doughnuts with Pomegranate Caramel

A couple of years ago, I took my son, Knight, to visit a friend's church. They were offering coffee and doughnuts afterwards. Knight was such a little guy that I didn't even know he knew the word 'doughnut', but suddenly he was like, 'I need more doughnut!'. I feel that way about doughnuts myself. I don't want them anywhere near me when I know I have to perform, as I have no self control when it comes to doughnuts. I make these when Knight and I want to indulge our cravings. I put a bourbon-based pomegranate glaze on them, but he likes a plain glaze; he's a classic kind of guy.

MAKES 10-12 DOUGHNUTS

3 × 7g sachets fast-action dried yeast

120ml hot water

940g plain flour, plus more for dusting

150g caster sugar

1½ teaspoons sea salt

115g white vegetable fat, softened at room temperature and diced

3 medium eggs

600ml boiling water

Rapeseed oil or vegetable oil for deep-frying

1 recipe Pomegranate Caramel (page 164)

1. Combine the yeast and the hot water in the bowl of a stand mixer fitted with a paddle attachment and set aside for 5 minutes to activate the yeast. Add 375g of the flour, the sugar and salt and mix on a low speed to combine, then add the shortening and mix to combine. Add the eggs one at a time, scraping down the bowl with a rubber spatula after each addition. Tip in the boiling water and blend well. Add the remaining flour and mix to combine. Increase the speed to medium and mix for 2 minutes until the dough is smooth and no longer sticks to the side of the bowl.

2. Take the bowl off the stand. Cover it with a tea-towel or kitchen paper and set aside in a warm place for 1 hour until the dough has risen to about double its size.

3. Lightly dust a flat work surface and your rolling pin with flour. Turn the dough out onto the work surface and roll it out until it is 1cm thick. Cut out 10-12 doughnuts with a doughnut cutter or a 5-7.5cm biscuit cutter. Place them on a baking tray, cover them with the tea-towel and set aside in a warm place to rise for 45 minutes.

4. Heat 5-7.5cm of oil in a medium saucepan over a medium heat until it reaches 180°C. Prepare a bed of kitchen paper for draining.

5. Drop the doughnuts into the oil and fry for 45 seconds-1 minute per side until golden brown. Remove the doughnuts from the oil and drain them on the kitchen paper. Drizzle them with the pomegranate glaze and serve warm. If not serving immediately, drizzle over some more glaze once you are about to serve.

Pomegranate Caramel

I love pomegranate seeds for their colour and flavour, and we grew up eating them – they were like little jewels. I use this caramel in two ways: as a doughnut glaze and also, without the butter, as a syrup for duck (see Peking Duck, page 103) or to drizzle on pancakes. Pomegranate seeds are a lot of work for such a little thing! They have a distinctive flavour that is great with the doughnuts.

MAKES ABOUT 360G

180g pomegranate seeds

4 allspice berries

4 whole cloves

1 cinnamon stick

220g soft light or dark brown sugar

360ml bourbon

¼ teaspoon cayenne pepper

115g unsalted butter, cut into cubes (use if making a glaze)

1. Combine the pomegranate seeds and 120ml water in a small saucepan and bring to the boil over a high heat.

2. Add the allspice, cloves, cinnamon stick and sugar. Return the liquid to the boil. Reduce the heat and simmer for about 10 minutes until the seeds are mushy and nearly all of the liquid has evaporated. Pour through a fine-mesh sieve into a medium bowl; discard the contents of the sieve and return the syrup to the saucepan.

3. Add the bourbon and bring the mixture to the boil over a high heat. Reduce the heat and simmer until thick and syrupy. Turn off the heat and stir in the cayenne to finish the syrup. If you are creating a glaze, add the butter and stir until it is thoroughly incorporated. Any remainder glaze can be stored in the fridge.

Pumpkin Mascarpone Spanakopita

This breakfast pastry is made with filo pastry, which you can buy frozen. It's so easy to work with, which makes this spanakopita really simple to put together, and yet it's such a special treat to serve to friends. I'm so into pumpkin, from bread to muffins, pancakes to soup, and we have a great choice from September through to March here in LA.

SERVES 8

1 butternut squash, about 900g, halved lengthways and seeds removed

140g unsalted butter, melted

½ teaspoon sea salt

280g mascarpone cheese, softened at room temperature

150g demerara sugar

1 teaspoon ground cinnamon

¼ teaspoon ground cloves

1 vanilla pod

Plain flour for dusting

450g (about 20 sheets) filo pastry, defrosted according to the packet instructions if frozen

1 medium egg beaten with 1 tablespoon water to make an egg wash

1. Position an oven shelf in the centre of the oven and preheat the oven to 190°C/gas mark 5.

2. Put the squash on a baking tray, cut sides up. Using a pastry brush, paint the cut sides with 25g of the butter and sprinkle lightly with the salt. Bake on the centre shelf for 45-55 minutes until the squash is tender. Set aside to cool slightly. Scoop the squash flesh out of the peel and into a large bowl; discard the peel. Mash the squash with a potato masher. Add the mascarpone, sugar, cinnamon and cloves. Split the vanilla pod down the middle with a paring knife and scrape the seeds into the filling. (Save the pod for another use; boil it in water for the world's best air freshener or put it in a jar of sugar to make vanilla sugar.) Mash the squash filling together until the ingredients are thoroughly combined and the filling is smooth.

3. Dust a flat work surface with flour and lay out one sheet of the filo pastry on it. Brush the filo with some of the remaining melted butter and lay another sheet of dough on top of it. Brush with more butter and continue in this way until you have stacked half of the sheets (about 10) of filo. Spread half of the squash mixture over the surface of the dough, leaving bare a 4cm border around the edges of the dough. Starting at a short edge, roll the dough up like a scroll. Lift it onto one half of an ungreased baking tray. Repeat, making another spanakopita roll using the remaining sheets of filo and squash mixture. Put the second roll on the baking tray with the first one. Brush the outsides of both rolls with the egg wash.

4. Bake the spanakopita on the centre shelf for 40-45 minutes until it is golden brown and crispy. Remove from the oven and set aside to cool for about 5 minutes before slicing. Cut each spanakopita into 5cm-wide slices and serve warm.

Cocktails
Coquito

This is my culture's version of egg nog, made with a mixture of sweetened condensed milk, evaporated milk, and coconut milk. You can buy it, but like egg nog, it's one of those things that's pretty much only available during the holiday season. It was something I was not allowed to drink as a kid because it contains rum, but I always remember it being part of the tradition.

INGREDIENT NOTE: Make sure you have true cinnamon (*Cinnomomum Zeylanicum*) rather than Cassia cinnamon (*Cinnamomum Cassia*) because it has better flavour and is healthier for you.

SERVES 4

400ml can coconut milk

397g can condensed milk

2 × 170g cans evaporated milk

2 egg yolks

Pinch of fine sea salt

¼ teaspoon Ceylon cinnamon powder, plus more for dusting

240ml Puerto Rican white rum

Ground cinnamon, to serve

1. Place everything in a blender, except the ground cinnamon, and process for 3 minutes on a high speed until the liquid is frothy. Serve chilled in tumblers, dusted lightly with a little extra cinnamon.

Kelis's Sangria

Sangria feels like summer to me and everyone drank it like water when I was living in Spain. I serve it all the time when I entertain at home. It's refreshing, delicious, and it looks really pretty in a big jug. Also it's perfect for a summer barbecue or a picnic. You can make a red version with strawberries, black grapes, and oranges, or a white one with white wine and thick slices of citrus fruits. I like entertaining so it's fun to be able to serve a good sangria.

SERVES 4-6

75cl bottle red wine (choose a mid-price Spanish red wine)

½ × 75cl bottle high-quality tequila or rum

400g granulated sugar

1 tablespoon pure vanilla extract

1 teaspoon ground nutmeg

1 teaspoon ground cinnamon

A handful of sprigs of fresh mint

Fresh cherries, grapes, sliced apples and orange wedges

75cl bottle sparkling mineral water, chilled

1. Combine the wine, tequila, sugar, vanilla, nutmeg and cinnamon in a large pan. Stir until the sugar has dissolved. Add the mint sprigs and fruit, cover and refrigerate for 1–2 hours to marinate the fruit. Just before serving, add the mineral water and transfer to a glass pitcher.

Index

It takes an army of extremely focused and skilled people to put together a project like this. We were on deadline, and this is my first book so there was so much to learn and so little time.

I want to say thank you to my husband for a million reasons but mostly because on the worst days you always tell me I'm good enough. Thank you, Knight, for your relentless honesty even when I don't ask if you liked it. I should say thank you to my sister Bean because you were officially my first taste tester when we were just little girls. I'd like to point out that you survived.

I need to say thank you, Steve. When I told you food was next for me you didn't run. You trusted me and you stood behind me and made this all happen. You're family now, man. Thank you, Geoff, for your undying diplomacy and willingness to laugh even in the 11th hour when anyone else would throw in the towel.

Thank you, Alexis, for putting up with me in every situation and always pointing out that we could eat churros. Thank you, Brittany, for being my sous chef before you had any idea what that meant or why this was happening to you.

To Kyle, thank you for taking a chance on me, this has meant the world to me: it's my biography on plates. And I'm so happy! Thank you, David, for your impeccable eye for delicious. You are legendary and it was such an honour to have you in my home and a part of this love project with me. Thank you, Anita, for your amazing designs. Thank you to Hannah for your attention to detail and your always beautiful artwork. Thank you, Robin, for bringing the finest bits to me. It was like playing dress up. Sophia, Sarah, and Jessica, thank you for your kitchen collaborations, getting the food in front of the camera, and making sure it was always beautiful in the process. Carolynn, thanks for your help bringing this book to life. Thank you, as always, Maisha, for making my hair as big as possible and Gaby, for make up. Thank you to Bronwyn and the Spice Station for always being hospitable and for being one of my favourite places to shop with or without the cameras!

Mum, I can't say thank you enough. But thank you.